£9.95

INCLUDING CHILDREN

A Practical Companion
to the Alternative Service Book

Susan Sayers

Mini-worksheets drawn by
Helen Herbert

Other drawings by
Arthur Baker

First published 1990
in Great Britain by
KEVIN MAYHEW LTD
Rattlesden
Bury St Edmunds, Suffolk IP30 0SZ

ISBN 0 86209 168 3

Cover by Andrew Bennett
Typesetting by Typestylers, Ipswich, Suffolk
Printed and bound in Hong Kong by Colorcraft Ltd.

Contents

HOLY WEEK

EASTER

PENTECOST

INTRODUCTION

Both children and adults form the people of God. All of us help and encourage one another on the Way. Each is special and essential. Jesus not only welcomed children but also used them to teach spiritual truths about our relationship with our heavenly Father.

Including Children, based on *Springboard to Worship*, grows out of the conviction that children have much to teach adults as well as the other way round. Our worship on Sundays needs to include all Christian pilgrims, regardless of size or date of birth!

Accordingly, the themes and readings of the day in *Springboard to Worship* are explored in terms of the whole people of God, including children. In response to popular demand, this book brings all the "children's teaching" parts together, with additional resources, for the convenience of those involved with children's ministry. It still remains an integral part of the whole worshipping community.

Children's activities during the Ministry of the Word cover the same ground as is covered by adults listening to the readings and sermon; whenever practical, the two are combined. So what the children produce will often clarify or bring into sharp focus some point the whole community has been thinking about. The music on a particular Sunday will be relevant to what everyone is studying; the worship will then draw all together.

The material is deliberately flexible. It is rare for any published teaching course to be exactly suitable for our own particular needs, and consequently there is always the temptation to cut people to fit the fabric! If children's ministry is to be a real part of Sunday worship, it will need to be fresh and relevant, springing from prayerful and enthusiastic preparation and input, where the character and experience of leaders are used to the full. After all, we are not so much in the business of teaching people facts about Jesus, as introducing them to him in person.

Don't let panic set in at this point! I am not suggesting that we gaily throw all teaching material away and are flung back on our own inspiration which may well refuse to come in the limited time we all have available. Rather the opposite. The whole purpose of this book is to give ideas, start you thinking, provide ways of getting across the truths and themes of the readings, suggest, encourage and teach. It may well be that as you read through each week's suggestions, other ideas occur to you. Great! Use them. Adapt the resources and alter them as much as you like, because they are there as a springboard — the diving you are free to do yourself!

It follows that prayerful preparation by everyone involved is of paramount importance and no amount of resources or ideas can be a substitute for this. *Springboard to Worship* includes weekly sections of notes on the readings and discussion questions to help here.

Including Children also has a series of weekly activity sheets. These are copyright-free and can be used as they stand, or you can select material you want. Copy them for the children to take home, use them in church, put them in the magazine or news sheet, distribute them at clubs or Bible study groups or use them in conjunction with your learning programme. There is only one thing they are *not* to be used for, and that is as a lazy substitute for real ministry!

You may find it useful to keep a record of what you actually do each week. Then, after following the two-year cycle of the A.S.B., you will have additional resources of your own to use in planning.

Starting from scratch?

If the Lord does not build the house,
the work of the builders is useless. (Psalm 127)

Begin with prayer. Ask the whole parish to pray. Then gather a small cluster of committed people and write down your real aims and needs. You may be surprised at what comes out of this valuable exercise; it helps us establish what our own faith is all about.

Present your aims and needs to the parish through the P.C.C./magazine/handout or whatever. The whole parish must feel involved right from the start — your task is not to take the children out of everyone's hair, but to include them more than ever before!

Now gather some people who are happy to help but not happy to lead. All together, plan the first few sessions in considerable detail so that everyone is confident about what to prepare or bring. Then advertise by individual invitation, including as many children in the parish as possible. Go personally to tell the Brownies and Cubs, Youth groups etc., and don't forget the local schools.

Have your meeting area set up in an attractive, thought-provoking, ordered way when the children come in . This positively affects their expectations and their behaviour. Then *enjoy* the time together. Let it be really lively and joyful and fun. Let it be quiet and thoughtful. Let it be challenging and hopeful. In other words, allow the Lord space to work, in the framework you have prepared. When you are all in church, spread the children around among the other worshippers so that they can be welcomed with love. Adults and children can then worship alongside each other. Have the children's work displayed clearly, so that as everyone gathers round the Lord's table, all his people share his love.

INCLUDING CHILDREN

9th SUNDAY BEFORE CHRISTMAS

Theme: The Creation

Year 1

Genesis 1:1-3, 24-31a; Colossians 1:15-20; John 1:1-14

Read the children the story of creation, either from the Bible, or from a Bible story book such as *God Makes the World*, (Palm Tree Press). In prayer together thank God for the wonderful world he has made for us. Then give out lumps of modelling clay and make some models of some of God's plants and creatures. Arrange everything on a large tray which has been covered with green and blue paper to represent the land and sea. Write a title for the display: GOD MADE THE WORLD, and bring it into the church for everyone to see. Try singing: *Fishes of the ocean* (Many Ways to Praise, 34); *Push little seed* (Many Ways to Praise, 6), *Who put the colours in the rainbow?* (Hymns Old and New, 584).

Year 2

Genesis 2:4b-9, 15-end; Revelation 4; John 3:1-8

On tables around the edge of the room put a varied collection of things created by God, together with hands-on activities. Let the children spend some time exploring these.

Display suggestions:

Assorted rocks and pebbles: How many colours can you see?
Sea shells: Put a shell to your ear. What can you hear?
Autumn leaves: Find which trees these came from, with a chart.
A globe: Can you find Britain? The Pacific Ocean? Australia?
Feathers: Look for the hooks on the end of the feathers with a magnifying glass.
Animal pictures or models: Which box does each animal belong to? (With boxes labelled "Meat eaters", "Grass eaters")
Prism or cut glass beads: Can you make rainbows?
Containers of sand, dried peas, bird seed, sheep's wool: Feel the different textures
Magnets and a box of things to test for magnetism: What will the magnet attract?

When everyone has sampled everything, gather in a circle to talk about the amazing world God has made for us to live in and look after. How can we look after it well? Thank God together for all he has made, and help the children write down their thanks to God for the things they find most amazing, beautiful, powerful or clever. Cut round the decorated prayers, stick double-sided sticky tape on the back and bring them into church. Try singing: *If I were an astronaut*, or, *There's a seed* (MWTP); or *If I were a butterfly* (ONA).

9 before Christmas (1) The Creation

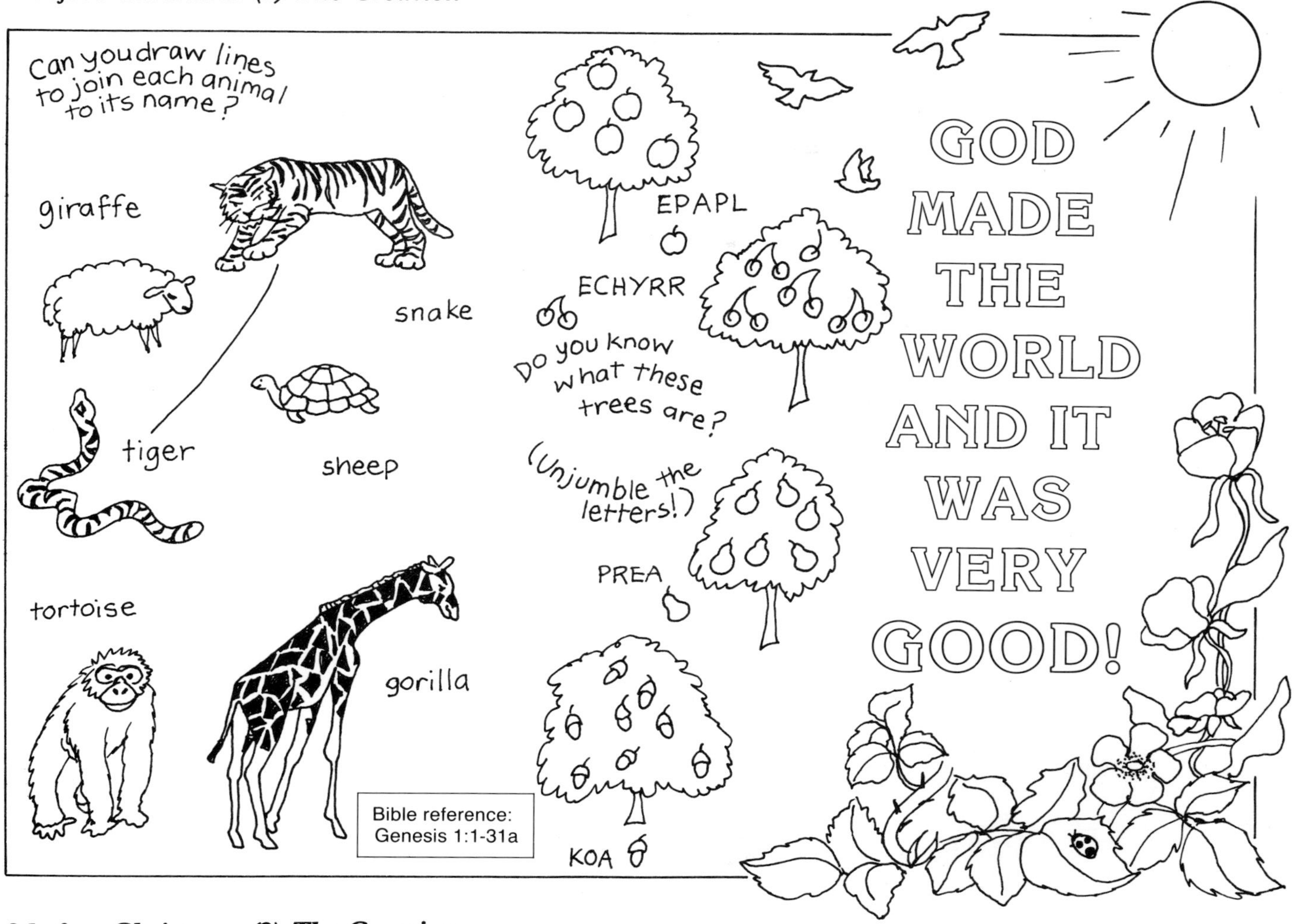
Can you draw lines to join each animal to its name?
giraffe
snake
tiger
sheep
tortoise
gorilla
EPAPL
ECHYRR
Do you know what these trees are? (Unjumble the letters!)
PREA
KOA
GOD MADE THE WORLD AND IT WAS VERY GOOD!

Bible reference:
Genesis 1:1-31a

9 before Christmas (2) The Creation

THEN GOD PLANTED A GARDEN AND THERE HE PUT THE MAN HE HAD MADE.
Which tree did God tell the man he must not eat?
THE
OF
IT
C
A
AT
OF
H
G
AND
D

A	D	M	O	U	S	E	I
I	M	W	B	J	B	R	U
T	N	A	H	P	E	L	E
E	C	S	R	E	A	K	T
L	S	P	D	F	R	N	G
C	E	B	O	O	Y	W	O
R	A	B	B	I	T	L	R
B	D	P	A	Y	F	Q	F

Can you find the names of these creatures?

ELEPHANT
BEAR
FLY
FROG
DEER
WASP
RABBIT
MOUSE

Genesis 2:4-end

8th SUNDAY BEFORE CHRISTMAS

Theme: The Fall

Year 1

Genesis 4:1-10, 1 John 3:9-18; Mark 7:14-23

Remind the children of the beautiful world God has made and then talk with them about the way we all sometimes spoil it. Have ready a display of pictures to help the thinking. Cut some from newspapers, or use these drawings:

Tell the children the story of how Cain started off being mean and ungrateful to God, became jealous of his brother, began to hate his brother and eventually killed him. Slide a stone down a tilted tray to show how easy it is to slide down once you've got started. Perhaps they have tried stopping halfway down a slide — it takes a lot of strength.

What can we do to stop ourselves slipping down into sin? Show them a large rolled strip of paper and ask one child to hold an end while another child unrolls it. The others read out what it says:

Hold on tight to Jesus

HOLD ON TIGHT TO JESUS!

We can talk to Jesus about our bad habits and ask him to help us change them.

We can call to him for strength when we feel tempted to be greedy, unkind or bad-tempered.

We can try to form new habits, such as being helpful, friendly or generous.

Pray together, thanking God for his gifts to us through the last week, asking his forgiveness for times we have spoilt his world, and offering him the coming week for God to use us to spread his love around.

Colour in the letters on the strip of paper and display it in church. Try singing:

Love is something if you give it away
When I needed a neighbour (ONA, 576)
Never let Jesus into your heart unless . . . (MWTP, 104)

Year 2

Genesis 3:1-15; Romans 7:7-13; John 3:13-21

Talk together about how difficult it is to be good. Even quite young children will have discovered the tiresome truth that Paul also found: the things we don't intend to do, we end up doing; and some of the good things we mean to do, don't get done! Such a discussion does not damage a child's self image; rather, it helps him see that doing wrong sometimes is part of being human, and the important thing is to say sorry and put things right quickly.

Now tell them a story of Adam and Eve being disobedient. This is a sin they will readily understand; they may also pick up the way Adam blames Eve and she blames the serpent. They had chosen not to do what God wanted, and that spoilt things. Help them see how we, too, are always free to choose whether to be loving or unloving. Who can help us make the right decision? Jesus can. Why? Show them a picture of Jesus healing, then teaching, so they can see that, though a man like Adam, Jesus was God's Son, and always, without fail, chose to be loving.

Even when people were horrid and cruel to him he went on loving. (Show them a crucifix.) Even when they killed him, he loved and forgave. So if we trust him as our most special friend, he will help us to grow more and more loving.

Using two spent matches and a wire bag-fastener, the children can make a small cross to carry about in a pocket, to remind them to ask Jesus to help when they are tempted to be unkind, mean or selfish.

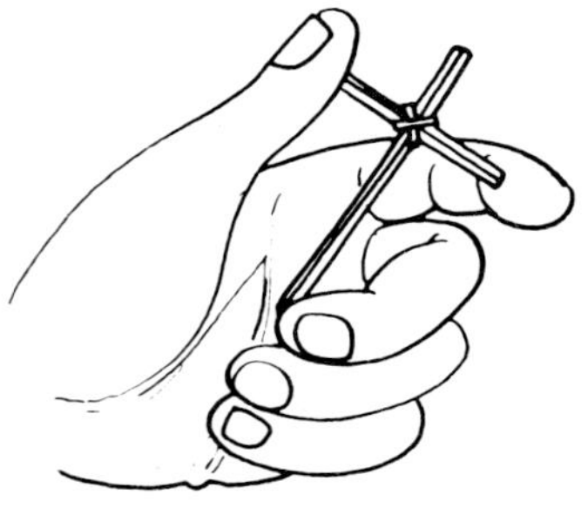

8 before Christmas (1) The Fall

IT'S GOD'S WORLD — sometimes we

SPOIL
it

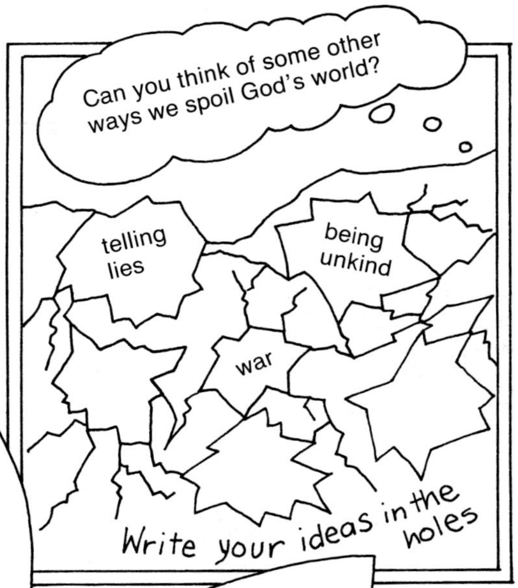
Can you think of some other ways we spoil God's world?
telling lies
being unkind
war
Write your ideas in the holes

Draw CAIN here

Draw ABEL here

MURDERED

Name: CAIN
Job:
Crime:
Motive:

Name: ABEL
Job:

Bible reference: Genesis 4:1-10

FOR PUTTING THINGS RIGHT
FIRST AID

How can we help put things right?

Choose four good ways and write them in the arrows.

★ HELPING CLEAR UP ★ TRYING TO UNDERSTAND
★ SAYING SORRY ★ HITTING BACK ★ BEING FRIENDLY ★ SHOUTING

8 before Christmas (2) The Fall

ADAM AND EVE DISOBEY GOD.

The serpent said to Eve

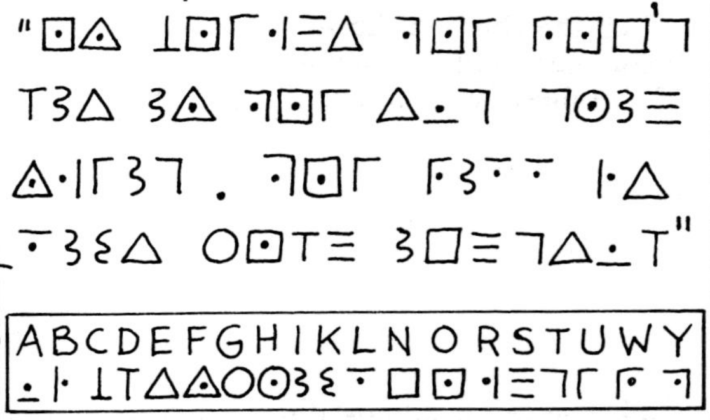
A B C D E F G H I K L N O R S T U W Y

But they weren't

Q. Who put things right?

A.

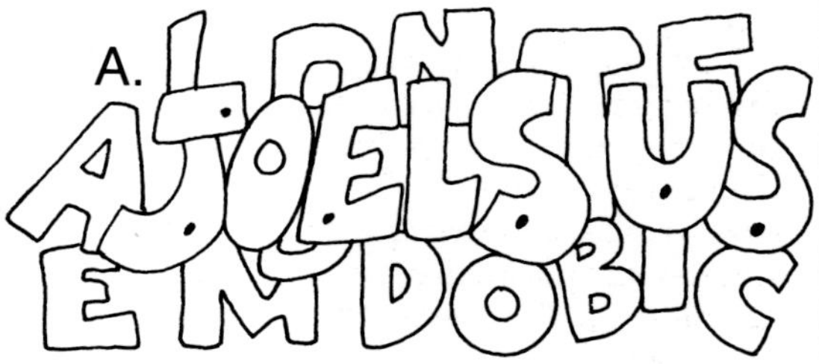

Colour the dotted letters

Genesis 3:1-15.

7th SUNDAY BEFORE CHRISTMAS

Theme: The Election of God's People — Abraham

Year 1

Genesis 12:1-9, Romans 4:13-end; John 8:51-end

First show the children a world map. Establish one or two countries they know of and then point out Haran and the route to Canaan. Also show pictures of the landscape there (the local library should have some books with photographs of the Bible lands). It is important that the children realise these places really exist!

Now tell the children about a man who lived there, called Abraham. Read them just the first paragraph of the Genesis reading. Talk together about how it feels to be starting out somewhere new for the first time, such as a new school, a new class or moving house. Abraham, too, may well have been a bit scared. He may not have particularly wanted to go. But he trusted God and obeyed him. God promised that he would be with Abraham and he kept his word.

Using an old baking tray, sand and stones, make a model of Abraham setting off for the promised land. Abraham and his family are made of pipecleaners and pieces of material, and sheep and goats are made from black and white pipe-cleaners. Write a title for the model:

ABRAHAM TRUSTED GOD

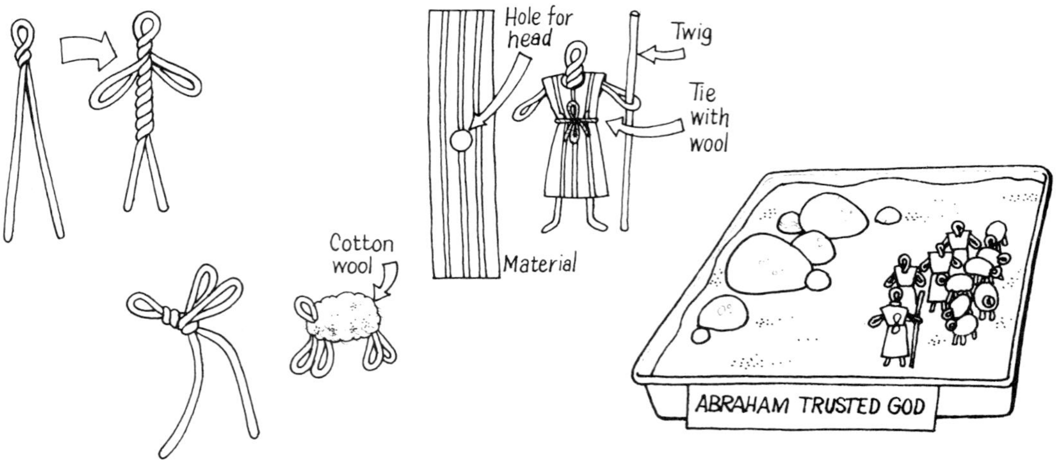
Hole for head
Twig
Tie with wool
Cotton wool
Material
ABRAHAM TRUSTED GOD

Year 2

Genesis 22:1-18, James 2:14-24 (25, 26) Luke 20:9-17

First show some pictures of people in different uniforms (nurses, soldiers, brownies, astronauts, etc.) and ask the children what each person is.

Have the labels ready and stick them on to the pictures as each is named. Talk about what we know about each one because of the uniform worn. (We know, for instance, that the nurse probably works in a hospital, takes temperatures, gives out medicine and changes bandages etc.)

Then show an ordinary group of people. They are Christians (put on label) but their uniform is not their clothes — it is the way they behave. We can't see their faith, but we can see the effect of their faith, in their behaviour.

Discuss with the children what marks a person as being a Christian who has faith in God. (They worship God, pray, behave lovingly, forgive quickly, are happy even when they don't get everything their own way, they are helpful and kind etc.)

Point out that often we don't behave like this, and then we are letting God down, just as a nurse would let the hospital and the patients down if she didn't give out the right medicines. If we say we believe in God then we must show our faith in the way we act.

Now read them the first paragraph of the reading from James 2, first dressing one child up in rags with a begging bowl, so that you call across to this child, 'Good luck to you,' etc. at the appropriate time. Afterwards collect ideas for how a person with real faith in God would help, and act this out.

Organise an event during the week in which they can all help someone in a practical way.

Suggestions:

- clearing leaves from paths of elderly people
- a sponsored silence in aid of a charity
- a visit to an old people's home to sing to the residents and chat to them

Try singing: *Wanted — Good hands* (MWTP, 50), *Forward in faith* (MWTP, 54).

ABRAHAM TRUSTED GOD.

To think about

How might you feel if God asked your family to leave the country and go to an unknown place?

Circle the ways you might feel:

nervous excited scared happy

angry sad worried relieved

Bible reference: Genesis 12:1-9

(Take 1st letter of each object)
Where did he start from?

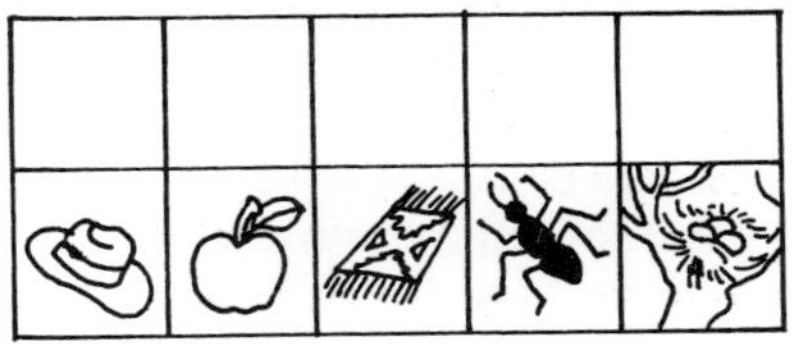

Where did he arrive?

The first thing Abraham did when he arrived was this:

THENBUILTONSAN
RANGALTARTHE
ATOSTHEILORD

COLOUR IN EACH DOTTED LETTER

GOD SAID TO ABRAHAM, 'NOW I KNOW THAT YOU TRUST ME!'

Genesis 22:1-18

Join the dots to see what God provided for the sacrifice in the end.

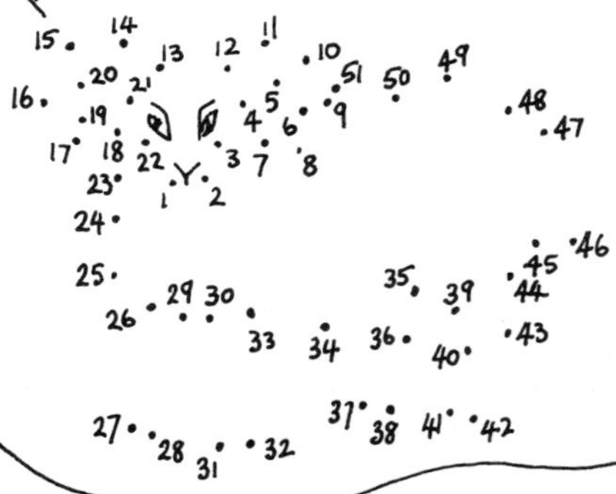

Which way to the hill for the sacrifice?

Jigsaw message

CAN
GOD
ALWAYS
TRUSTED
BE

6th SUNDAY BEFORE CHRISTMAS

Theme: The Promise of Redemption — Moses

Year 1

Exodus 3:7-15; Hebrews 3:1-6; John 6:25-35

Talk with the children about what they have eaten for breakfast. Then say something like: 'Well, you won't be needing any more food today, then, will you.' Pretend to be surprised that they are expecting to have more food later on. Why? Because they will get hungry again.

Now show the children a picture of Jesus feeding the 5,000 with bread and fish. Everyone had enough to eat at the time. But would they get hungry again? Yes; one loaf will not keep us alive for ever. Jesus told the people that he was like a loaf of bread — not to keep our bodies alive but to feed the spirit part of us which can live for ever. If we have Jesus living in us we shall never be spiritually hungry again; he will keep us full of love, peace and joy.

Whenever we eat bread we can remember that we need Jesus, our bread of life as well. Help the children make this bread basket to use at home, and pop a roll into each to eat with their lunch.

Jesus is the bread of life

Year 2

Exodus 6:2-8; Hebrews 11:17-31; Mark 13:5-13

Remind the children about Abraham, who was called by God to leave his home city and travel to the Promised Land. Explain how, many generations later, the people of Israel settled in Egypt during a long drought; how the Egyptians later began using them as slaves and treating them badly.

(This should be very brief, but it is important for the children to begin to see the 'shape' of God's plan for salvation, rather than a number of unconnected events.)

Show the children a picture of Moses as a baby, hidden in his basket. This was to be the person God had chosen to lead his people to freedom. When he grew up God told him that he had heard his people's groaning and crying, and was going to help them and set them free. (With older children read the Exodus passage here.) Moses trusted God, and God kept his promise.

Food in the Desert (Palm Tree Press) emphasises the growth of faith through the hardships in the wilderness. Read this to the children, showing them all the pictures, to give them an idea of how God can be trusted, and how he kept his promise to Moses and his people.

Have ready the separate letters of GOD CAN BE TRUSTED on sheets of thin card, and a length of string. Give the letters out for the children to decorate and cut out, punch two holes in the top of each letter, and string them up in the right order so that the unjumbled message appears. If possible, let the children bring this into church and hang it up between two chairs, so that everyone can see.

Try singing:

Put your hand in the hand
Moses I know you're the man (ONA, 327)
Think big (ONA, 524).

6 before Christmas (1) The Promise of Redemption — Moses

GOD SAID TO MOSES, 'I WILL BE WITH YOU!'

Exodus 3:7-15

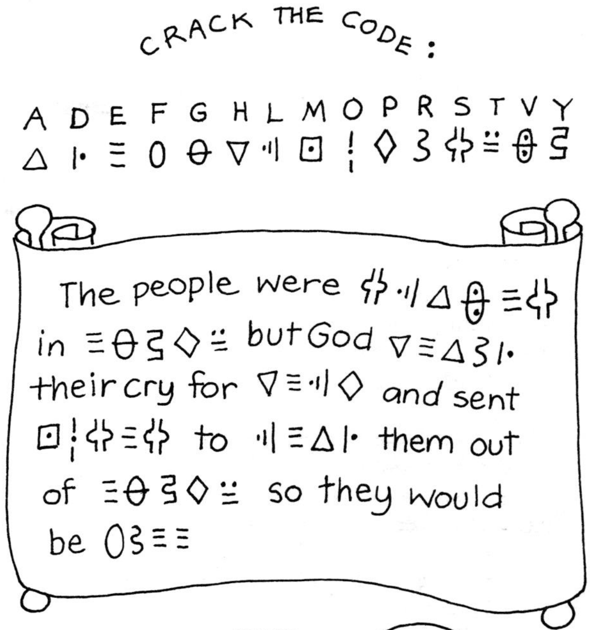

CRACK THE CODE:
A D E F G H L M O P R S T V Y
The people were
in
but God
their cry for
and sent
to
them out
of
so they would
be

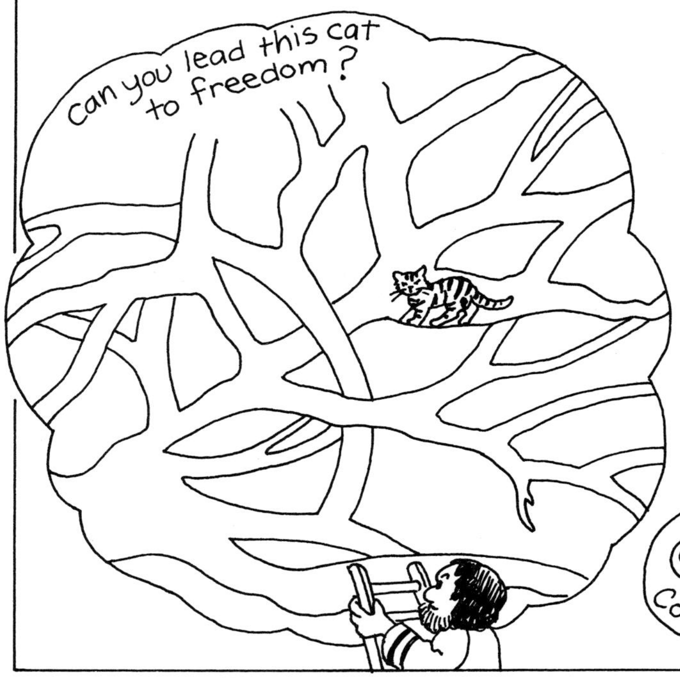

can you lead this cat to freedom?

Jesus leads us out of slavery, too ~ he sets us

OFTREELEPHFAROOLME
ASHIENO

Colour the dotted letters

6 before Christmas (2) The Promise of Redemption — Moses

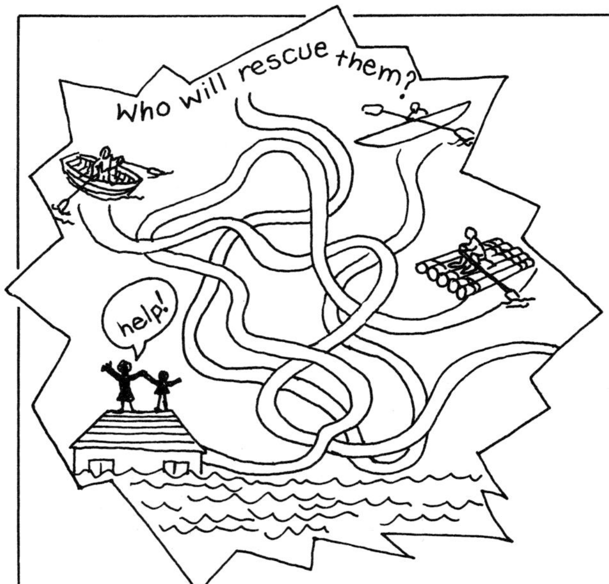

Who will rescue them?
help!

GOD TOLD MOSES 'I WILL RESCUE MY PEOPLE!'

We can always:

STROUSTINGSOLDO
ATBOOKHAECLIPPING
BUSY

colour the dotted letters

S	E	G	B	O	A	L	R
A	M	S	T	P	Y	G	E
P	S	O	I	C	G	P	S
E	L	J	S	M	B	L	C
O	A	C	H	E	O	F	U
P	V	N	K	E	S	R	E
L	E	A	D	R	D	C	P
E	S	E	R	F	I	M	Q

Find these words from the story:

MOSES
RESCUE
SLAVES
EGYPT
PROMISE
FREE
LEAD
PEOPLE

Exodus 6:2-8

5th SUNDAY BEFORE CHRISTMAS

Theme: The Remnant of Israel

Year 1

1 Kings 19:9-18; Romans 11:13-24; Matthew 24:37-44

Have ready three parcels, wrapped up in Christmas paper. They should all be the same size and shape — ask a shoe shop to let you have some shoe boxes. Inside one box place a lot of wadding, tissue or scrunched-up newspaper, in another place a tiny jewellery box containing something precious, such as a gold ring, or a diamond. In the third, place a pair of shoes.

Talk with the children about preparing our parcels for Christmas, and the fun of surprises. It is exciting to see a parcel with our name on it and not know what is inside. Often it turns out to be different from what we expect. Now show them the three parcels. Do they think that because they look the same they will have the same things inside? Ask one child to undo the first parcel. At the shoe box stage, guess the contents. When they see all the paper they will still expect something to be tucked inside. It's a surprise to find nothing there. Ask another child to open the second parcel. At the shoe box stage this time some may still expect shoes. Others will expect nothing. This time the contents are much more precious than we expected. A third child opens the last parcel. Stop again at the shoe box stage. Very few will now expect shoes, so it comes as a surprise to find what would normally be expected in a shoe box.

God is full of surprises, too. Sometimes, sadly, we may expect to find him in the lives of people who claim to follow him, but their behaviour shows that he isn't there. (Perhaps others may not find him in OUR behaviour, sometimes.) At other times he surprises us by blessing us richly when we are not expecting it. (On a bad day, when everyone seems cross with you, your pet gives you a special welcome, perhaps.)

We need to keep looking out for God, not just tucking him away into Sunday mornings. Otherwise, when he comes again we won't be ready for him. Read the last paragraph of today's Gospel and pray together that God will help us all stay faithful in our lives.

Help the children make these traffic lights to remind them.

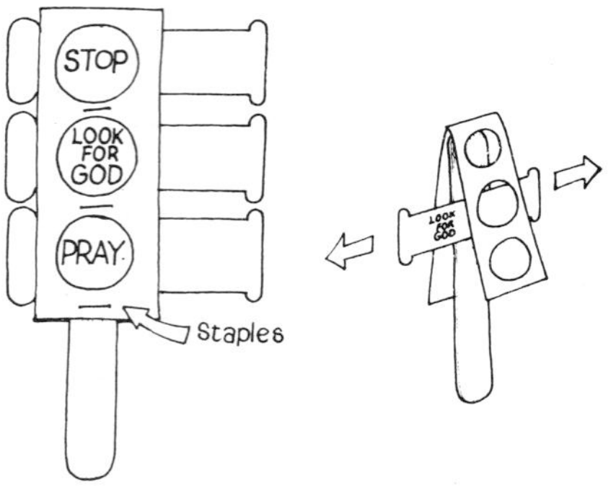
STOP
LOOK FOR GOD
PRAY
Staples

Try singing: *In joy sing of his love* (MWTP, 64), *Love one another* (MWTP, 52).

Year 2

Isaiah 10:20-23; Romans 9:19-28; Mark 13:14-23

Bring in a box of pencils or crayons, most of which are blunt or broken. (In my experience such collections are easy to find!) Ask two or three children to pick out of the box the pencils and crayons which are sharp and unbroken. Out of all that box only a very few were still in a good state. Explain today's readings by referring to the pencils. In a way we are like the pencils, except that we are able to go and get ourselves sharpened and cleaned up when we need to. (Saying sorry to God when we have been selfish or unkind, and making an effort to put things right again.) We can also choose not to bother. But we never know when God is wanting to use us, and if we have let ourselves get into a bad state, he won't be able to use us very easily. It's not enough to be a pencil — we need to be SHARPENED pencils.

On a chart or blackboard write down some ways we can make sure we are keeping ourselves ready. Here are some suggestions, but the children will have ideas as well:

Talking to Jesus and listening to him
Reading the Bible and learning from it
Putting things right quickly when we do wrong
Forgiving people when they hurt us or spoil our toys

Give the children a new pencil each and help them make this pencil-end for it.

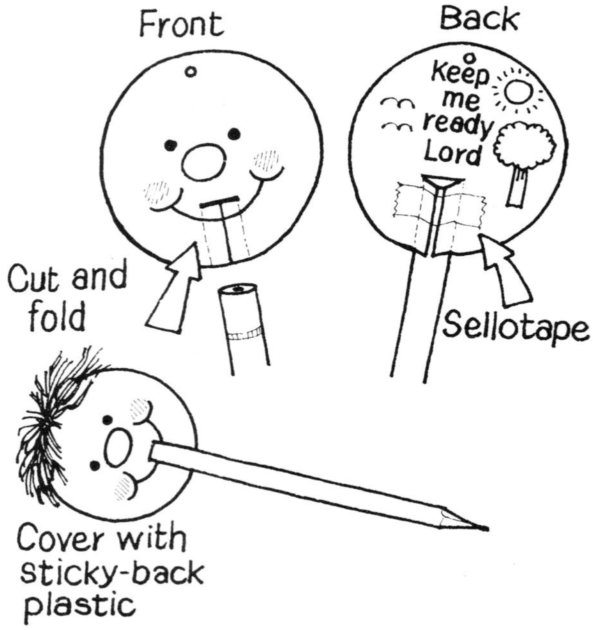
Front
Back
Keep me ready Lord
Cut and fold
Sellotape
Cover with sticky-back plastic

While they work, pass round some pencil sharpeners and let each child sharpen one of the blunt pencils. Try singing: *Give me joy in my heart; Shout aloud for Jesus* (MWTP, 58); *The builders* (MWTP, 30)

Can you keep faithful to the end of this path?
Well done!
When
JAM
felt he was the only faithful one left, God
him.

'KEEP AWAKE, THEN . . .
HOLD YOURSELVES READY.'

Matthew 24:37-44

'YOU ARE MY PEOPLE;
I LOVE YOU!' Romans 9:25

How can you stay faithful?

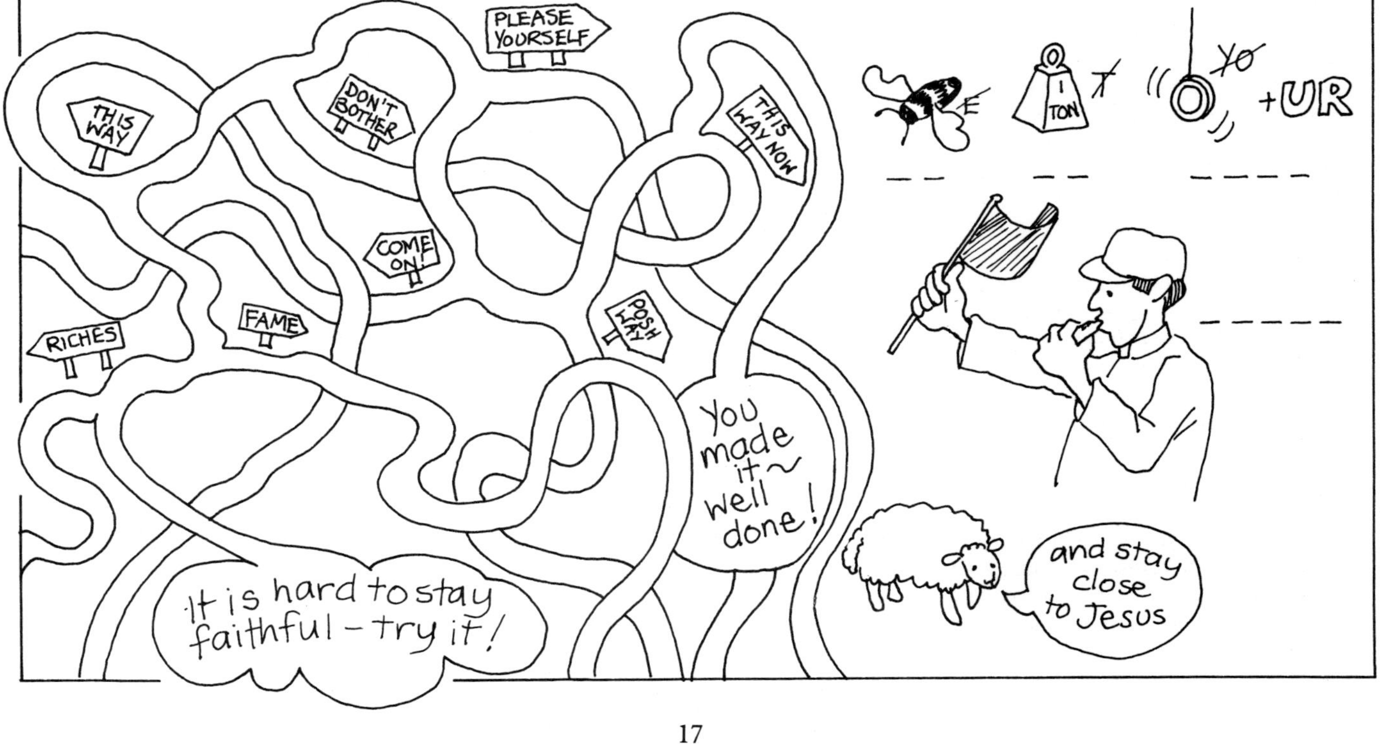
PLEASE YOURSELF
THIS WAY
DON'T BOTHER
THIS WAY NOW
COME ON!
POSH WAY
RICHES
FAME
You made it ~ well done!
It is hard to stay faithful – try it!
1 TON
+UR
and stay close to Jesus

1st SUNDAY IN ADVENT

Theme: The Advent Hope

Year 1

Isaiah 52:7-10; 1 Thessalonians 5:1-11; Luke 21:25-33

Bring in an alarm clock with a really loud ring or buzz. First talk to the children about how lovely it is when you're all warm and asleep in bed in the morning and then suddenly: BRRRRRRR! shatters your peace. Talk about how alarm clocks jerk you awake so you can get ready and not miss the day's activities. Advent (which means 'coming') is like an alarm clock, nudging us to get ready for Christ's coming. Tell them that as well as coming as a baby at Christmas time, 1,990 years ago, Jesus will come again one day with glory and power. We don't know when it will be, so we must be ready for him.

Now read the first paragraph of today's Gospel. You may feel the Good News translation is better suited to children's understanding — it is worth reading a few different versions to choose one most suitable for your particular group.

How can we get ready for Jesus?

Have written on a chart or blackboard:

1. Find out more about him — reading and praying
2. Try to live the Jesus way — being loving and kind.

If you do not have a church library for children this is a good time to start one. Give each child a card to record which book is read, and ask them to read four Bible story books during Advent. (Families may like to read them together.) On the back of each card print this prayer which the children can decorate. Encourage them to say their prayer each day through Advent.

Loving Father
help us to get ourselves READY
so we can welcome JESUS
with JOY
Name..................
Books I have read in
ADVENT

Try singing:

You can't stop rain from falling down (ONA, 594)
When the Lord returns (MWTP, 73)

Year 2

Isaiah 51:4-11; Romans 13:8-end; Matthew 25:31-end

Tell the children that Advent means 'coming', and remind them that in these weeks before Christmas we are getting ourselves ready for the coming of Jesus, not just as a baby at Christmas time but also the time when he will come again in great glory. We know this will happen because Jesus told us about it, but we don't know when, so we need to be prepared all the time.

With the aid of pictures and/or items of uniform, talk about people who always have to keep themselves ready because they don't know when their help will be needed — such as firemen, police, emergency staff at a hospital, lifeboatmen etc. How do they make sure they are ready?

— by practising rescues
— by keeping themselves fit
— by keeping their equipment well-oiled and repaired

Now read today's Gospel, asking the children to listen out for ways we can get ourselves ready for Jesus' coming. Have the different examples ('When I was hungry, you gave me food' etc) already written out on pieces of card, so that when they are mentioned after the reading you can display them.

Produce an empty carton and place all the cards inside, explaining that all these things are part of LOVING. (Write this in large letters on the carton.) Have some other pieces of card available and help the children write and decorate other practical ways of showing a caring love to others, such as offering to help Mum and Dad, sharing toys with others, being friendly to a child at school who is often lonely, or being pleased at someone else's success.

Carry the carton up to the altar at the offertory, and let the children process to the altar and put their card into the box. If there is time, these could be read out for the congregation to hear. They are offered along with the collection.

Try singing:

Love is something if you give it away
When the Lord returns (MWTP, 73)

Advent 1 (1) The Advent Hope

NOW IS THE TIME TO WAKE OUT OF SLEEP!

He's coming
How lovely on the mountains are the feet of the herald who brings good news! Isaiah 52:7

What is the good news?

Romans 13:11

Colour in the dotty bits

Advent 1 (2) The Advent Hope

It is time for you to wake out of sleep

Jesus is coming In all God's glory!

Draw in the faces

How will Jesus want to find us behaving? ring the "Yes", cross out the "No"
with forgiveness
with kindness
with anger
with meanness
with greed
with sharing
with love
with jealousy

Romans 13:8-end

2nd SUNDAY IN ADVENT

Theme: The Word of God in the Old Testament

Year 1

Isaiah 55:1-11; 2 Timothy 3:14-4:5; John 5:36b-end

Set up a treasure hunt with clues which direct the children from one place to another, like this:

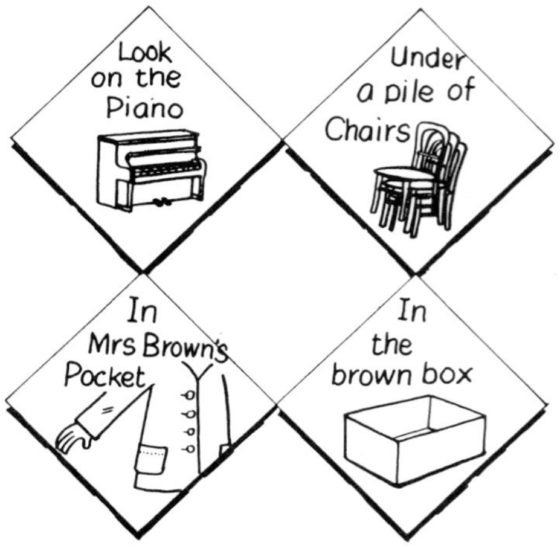
Look on the Piano
Under a pile of Chairs
In Mrs Brown's Pocket
In the brown box

The 'treasure' is a torch or bicycle lamp. Switch it on and talk with the children about how useful it is in helping us find our way in the dark, without tripping over things or causing accidents.

Now show them several different Bibles, explaining that in the Bible there are lots of clues to direct us to find the light of the world — Jesus. Give out these clues to different children and help them find the places which lead us to Jesus. You could have these already written up on a sheet of paper, each text covered with a question mark until the child finds the reference in the Bible: Listen to John the Baptist (Mark 1:7); Hear what God said (Mark 1:11); Where does the Spirit settle (Mark 1:10).

Dear Parents,
Help your child to notice
things that lead us to God
Thank you
Sunday
Monday
Tuesday
Wednesday
Thursday
Friday
Saturday
What did you hear, see, or read that led you to Jesus
Please bring back next week !!!!

Tell the children that there are lots of other clues every day which can lead us to Jesus, such as the beautiful and amazing things in nature, kind or unselfish behaviour; Bible stories and stories of the saints, help given when we need it, songs and poems etc.

Give the children this duplicated paper with a picture of Jesus in the centre which they can colour in. Then each day of the week they fill in one circle either with words or a drawing, with something that has directed them to think of Jesus and know him better. Ask them to bring these back next week.

Year 2

Isaiah 64:1-7; Romans 15:4-13; Luke 4:14-21

So as to get across the idea of fulfilled prophecy, make a 'scroll' by rolling a sheet of paper stuck on to sticks at either end, with a ribbon or tape on it for fastening. If possible, copy a little Hebrew writing on to it, as well as the prophecy included in today's gospel, (Isaiah 61:1-2a).

Show it to the children, ask them to guess what it is, and explain how, many years before Jesus was born, some people (prophets) were used by God to be messengers. Through them, God told his people that one day he would send someone very important who would save them and show them the right way to live. What they said was written down on scrolls like this one.

Ask one of the older children to read the first part of today's gospel, up to the point when Jesus is handed the scroll. Let one of the younger children hand the reader the home-made scroll. The passage from Isaiah 61:1-2a is read from it. The teacher now tells the last part of the gospel, with the children acting it out.

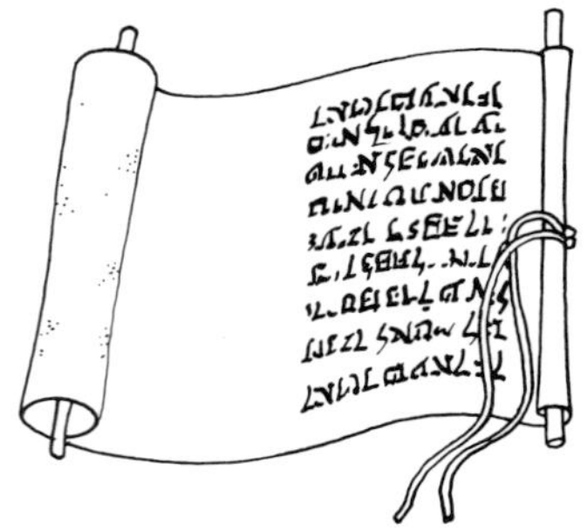

Recap with them about the kind of things the promised Saviour would do, matching them up bit by bit with what they know of Jesus. Have lots of pictures, Bible story books, and an illustrated Bible available to refer to. The children will be able to see that the prophecy really was coming true in Jesus.

Help the children make their own scrolls, with the prophecy stuck on. Garden canes, cut to size, make inexpensive sticks, and the paper is best attached with strong glue. Try singing: *All of the people* (MWTP, 39).

'Come, all who are thirsty, and drink!' Isaiah 55.1-11
I am your God and I love you!
Please yourself for today!
Get your own back on him!
only work if you get paid!
Which one is completely satisfying?

THE WORDS OF SCRIPTURE TELL US ABOUT GOD

Isaiah 55:1-11

L	E	O	J	A	M	P	H
H	S	O	C	L	G	A	F
J	E	R	E	M	I	A	H
R	S	B	I	A	D	M	O
U	O	Q	S	J	V	O	S
W	M	I	T	E	K	S	E
S	H	A	C	I	M	N	A

All these people wrote in the library that we call The Bible':

MOSES
ISAIAH
AMOS
JEREMIAH
JOEL
HOSEA
MICAH

The Old Testament was written in

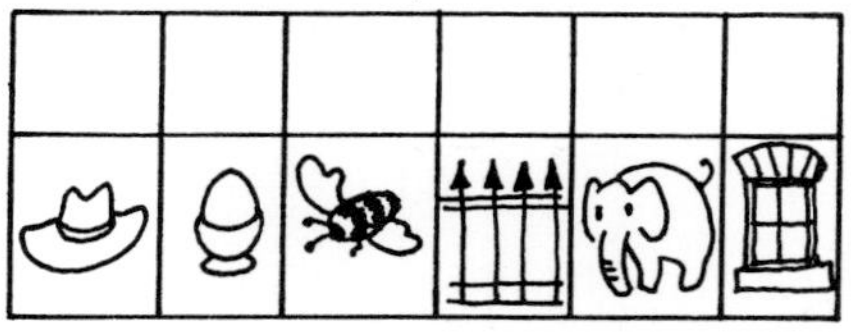

'TODAY', SAID JESUS, 'THIS WORD OF SCRIPTURE HAS COME TRUE.'

Luke 4:14-21

follow the strings to fit the words in

THE OLD TESTAMENT...
how
people
tells
his
God
and
the
of
....
us
the
his
know
made
led
to
ways
world
love

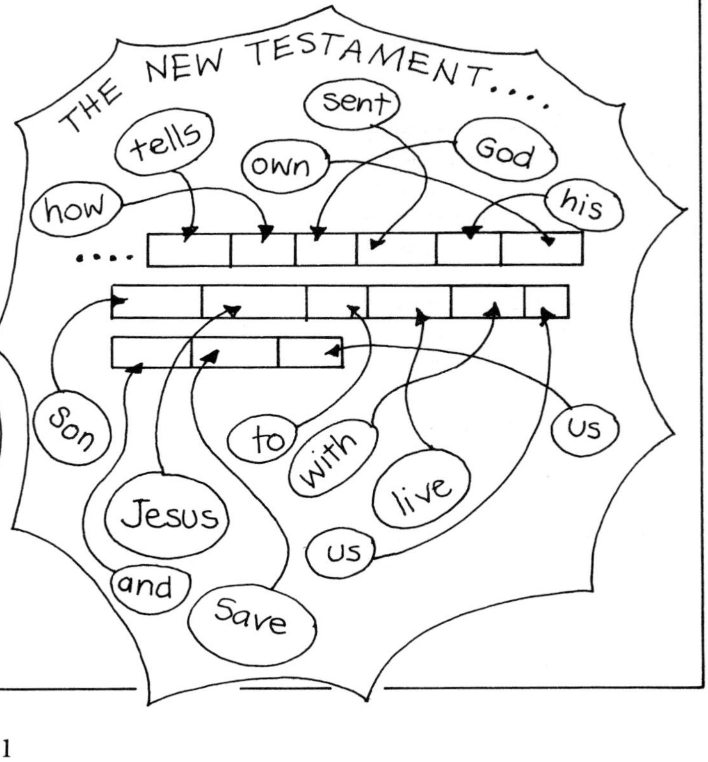
THE NEW TESTAMENT....
sent
tells
own
God
how
his
....
Son
to
with
us
Jesus
live
us
and
Save

3rd SUNDAY IN ADVENT

Theme: The Forerunner

Year 1

Isaiah 40:1-11; 1 Corinthians 4:1-5; John 1:19-28

First talk with the children about how their town or country prepares its streets for important visitors such as royalty, a winning football team or a film star. There may be flags hung up, streamers waving, a red carpet rolled out on the pavement and flowers planted round all the lamp posts for instance. If you have any photographs of such events, or a local carnival, show them around.

Now read them Isaiah 40:3-5 and the first part of today's Gospel, where John the Baptist uses the prophecy to explain his own job. Unroll a length of white material, about a yard wide and four yards long. (A double sheet split down the middle and joined end to end makes the right size: it is important that it looks big.)

The children are going to turn this strip of boring material into a highway for Jesus. At Christmas time it can be laid down in church so that when the Christ child is brought to the manger he is carried along the children's highway.

Have ready plenty of colourful oddments of material, a really efficient fabric glue, scissors, pens and templates. Discuss ways in which we can prepare ourselves for Jesus, and write these at intervals along the highway with coloured pens. On flower shapes they can write thank you messages.

Year 2

Malachi 3:1-5; Philippians 4:4-9; Matthew 11:2-15

Have ready a display of some of the lovely things in our world which enrich our lives and make us thankful. These may include water and food, pictures of the seasons and nature, warmth and light (candles) and photographs of people. Begin with thanks and praise for the God who loves us and gives us so much.

Then, using pictures from an illustrated Bible, tell the children about John the Baptist, sent by God to help people get ready for the Lord's coming. Many listened to what he said and made a big effort to change into more caring, honest and thankful people. As a sign that they were washed clean from evil, John waded into the river Jordan with them and prayed over them while they were dipped in the clean water. This was called Baptism. Remind the children that among those John baptised was Jesus himself. John recognised Jesus as being the Lord.

But then Herod had John arrested and thrown into prison, where he was chained up all on his own. He heard stories about what Jesus was doing and was surprised. He had expected the Lord to unite everyone in a great body that would drive out the Romans so the country would once more be free. Instead, Jesus was talking about loving our enemies, caring for one another — even foreigners — and he seemed to be making friends with bad people as well as good. Could this Jesus really be the Lord?

Poor John must have felt anxious, miserable and muddled. So he sent some of his own followers to Jesus to ask him straight out: 'Are you the one who is to come, or are we to expect some other?'

Jesus understood John's doubts. He thought of the best way to put John's mind at rest. (At this point get out the scroll used last week.) He knew that John had read the prophets' writings again and again and knew them inside out. So he quoted to John's messengers the prophecy about the blind receiving their sight, the lame walking and the lepers being made clean. The messengers could see that Jesus was making all this come true! John would understand that Jesus' kingdom was to come about by loving rather than fighting, however good the cause.

Help the children make up these figures for a flannelgraph, by colouring, cutting out and mounting on felt. Then, with the children putting the figures on to the flannelgraph, go through the main points of today's teaching.

1.
2.
3.
4.
5.
6.

A VOICE CRIES IN THE WILDERNESS, 'PREPARE THE WAY OF THE LORD.'

Isaiah 40:1-11

Draw in a straight road being made here~
You will have to level the route first

John the Baptist lived in the . He ate and wild . He baptised people in the as a sign that they were sorry, and wanted 2 right with God.

. . . and whose voice did cry in the wilderness 'Prepare the way of the Lord'? It was

WATERJOWATERHNWATERTHEWATER
BAWATERPTIWATERST

(cross out each WATER to find out)

'I AM SENDING MY MESSENGER WHO WILL CLEAR A PATH BEFORE ME'

Malachi 3:1-5

Join the dots, then colour the picture

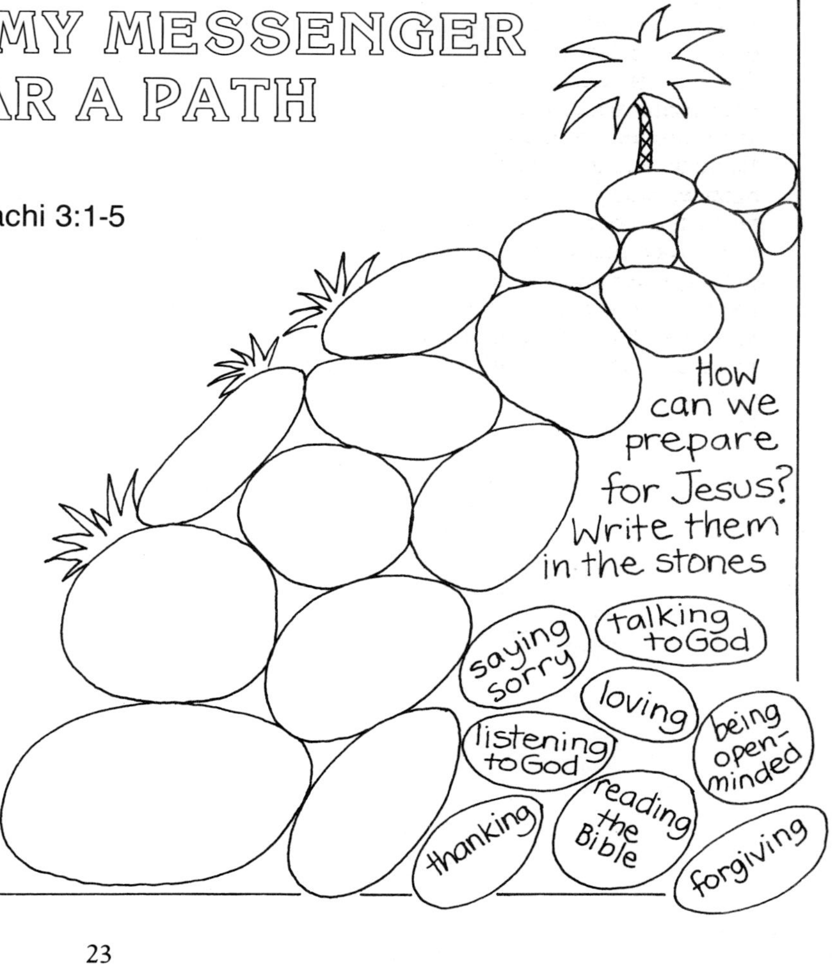
How can we prepare for Jesus? Write them in the stones
saying sorry
talking to God
loving
being open-minded
listening to God
reading the Bible
thanking
forgiving

4th SUNDAY IN ADVENT

Theme: The Annunciation

Year 1

Isaiah 11:1-9; 1 Corinthians 1:26-end; Luke 1:26-38a

Beforehand, prepare a picture of some houses in a street drawn on thin card, and cut round the doors so that they open and close. Also make a simple wooden-spoon or mop puppet.

First talk with the children about any good news they would like to share, and choose someone to knock on the door of each house to tell their news.

At the first house let the puppet say: 'Go away — I'm busy! at the second house: 'Pardon? . . . pardon? . . . I can't hear a word!'; at the third house: 'You don't expect me to believe THAT, do you?'; and at the fourth house: 'Hallo! Nice to see you . . . oh really? How lovely!' Discuss with them the different ways of receiving news, and how we need to welcome Jesus when he speaks to us, instead of being deaf, or too busy, or not believing what he says.

Now show the children a picture of God's messenger bringing some very important news to Mary. Who was the messenger? What was his news? Think back to the ways people sometimes react — did Mary say she was too busy, or couldn't hear, or didn't believe the angel? Read together the way Mary listened carefully and said she would certainly let God's will be done in her.

Unfold the children's 'highway' now (as prepared last week), and complete it by adding Mary's words. Use them as a prayer to make them part of our own preparation for the coming of Jesus into our lives.

Year 2

Zechariah 2:10-end; Revelation 21:1-7; Matthew 1:18-23

Talk about all the things they are doing ready for Christmas, and remind them of what we are all getting ready to celebrate — Jesus' birthday. Tell the children about how Mary and Joseph would be getting ready: packing food and clothing for their journey to Bethlehem, loading up their donkey, bringing baby clothes in case the baby arrives while they are away from home etc. Have some bags of nuts and raisins, dry biscuits, brightly coloured rugs, baby clothes and swaddling (length of sheeting). Put these out on the table as you discuss the things Mary and Joseph needed, and let the children pack them into cloth bags.

Now help them to make a small crib to put up in their homes, with a candle to light. Below is a pop-up version to try. The children will need scissors, glue and colouring pencils. Perhaps the finished crib could be offered at the altar before being taken home.

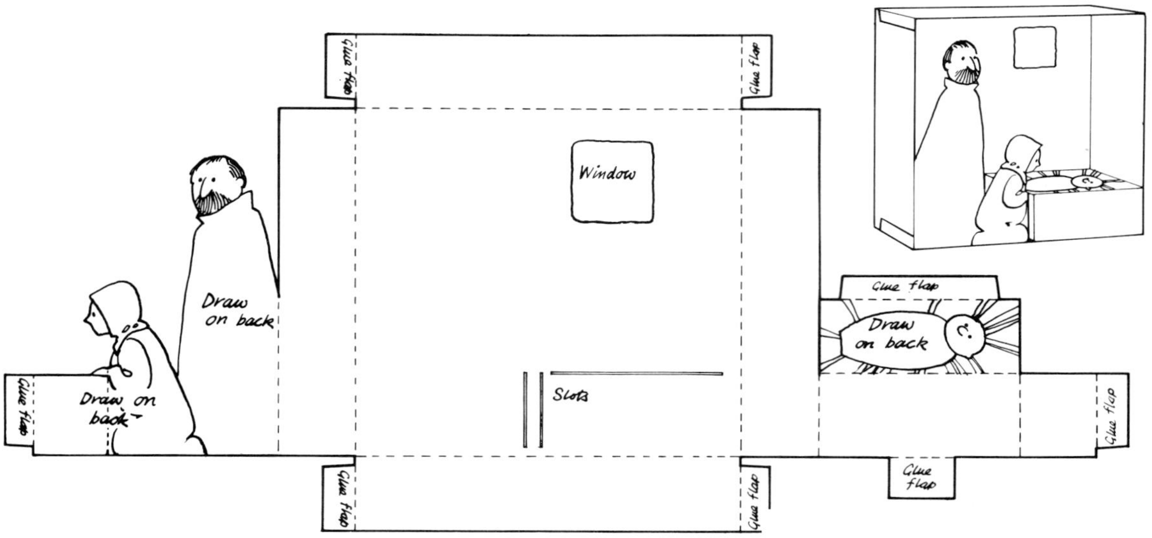
Glue flap
Window
Draw on back
Draw on back
Slots
Glue flap
Draw on back

Advent 4 (1) The Annunciation

'DO NOT BE AFRAID, MARY, YOU WILL HAVE A SON AND HIS NAME WILL BE JESUS!'

Luke 1:26-38

Join the dots, then colour the picture

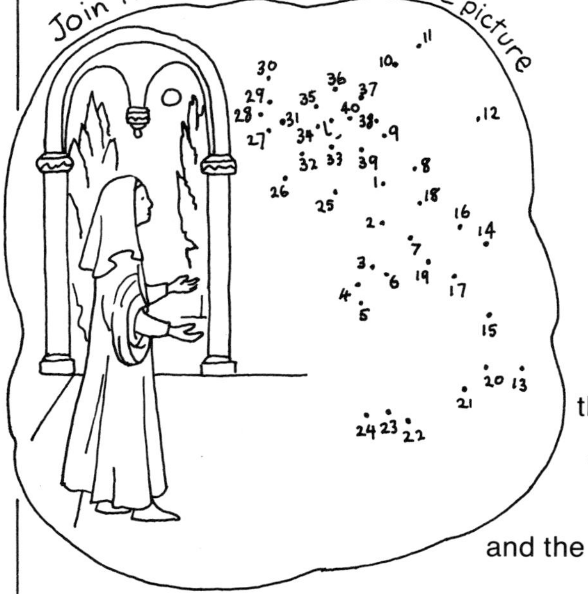

A	G	D	G	D	H	N	S
Y	A	T	E	O	K	A	P
R	B	C	N	N	V	T	L
A	R	H	P	E	S	O	J
M	I	Y	B	F	S	I	L
Q	E	O	B	M	I	D	E
W	L	J	R	A	S	O	T
T	A	S	O	N	B	G	V

MARY was engaged to JOSEPH. The angel GABRIEL was SENT from God to her. He TOLD her she would have a BABY who would be the SON of GOD. He would SAVE people from their sins. Mary said, LET all this be DONE, just as God has SAID.

Isaiah looked for a time when

the  will lie ⇩ 

and the  lie ⇩ with the 

Advent 4 (2) The Annunciation

Mary will have a son and his name will be Jesus!

Matthew 1:18-23

The prophets said this child would be known as

EMMANUEL

colours: R = red, O = orange, Y = yellow

which means

GOD WITH US

Jigsaw message!

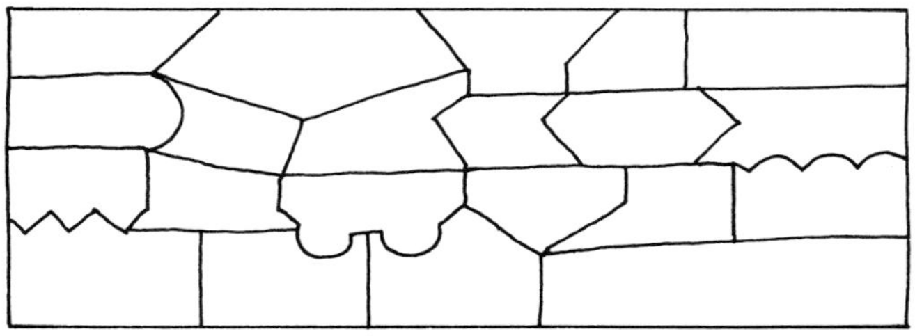

Revelation 21:1-7

will · wipe · God · them; · himself · be · with · he · away · and · from · their · tear · every · death · shall · eyes · more · no · be · will

CHRISTMAS

Theme: Christ is born

Years 1 and 2

Isaiah 9:2,6-7 or 62:10-12 or Micah 5:2-4; Titus 2:11-14; 3:3-7 or Hebrews 1:1-5 (6-12) or 1 John 4:7-14; Luke 2:1-14 (15-20) or 2:8-20 or John 1:1-14

Many churches find the Christingle symbolism helpful; leaflets providing an outline of Christingle, using the traditional orange (as the world) and candle (as the light of Christ) can be obtained from The Children's Society, Old Town Hall, Kennington Road, London SE11 4QD.

It is important that children feel part of the family worship at the festival. Perhaps they could have practised a special carol which they can sing during the service, or they may present a nativity play or tableau during or just after the Gospel.

Elderly residents in nursing homes love to hear children singing, too. If cards are made and distributed at the same time, the children will be providing a most valuable ministry.

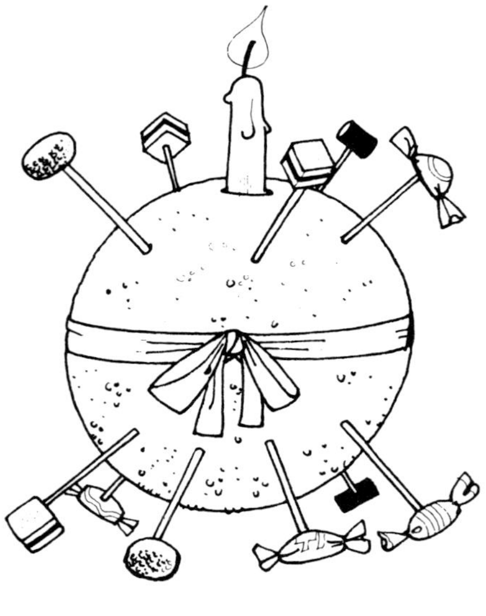

Christmas Day (1/2) Christ is born

I BRING YOU GOOD NEWS OF GREAT JOY!
Luke 2:1-14
God's gift to us
NOEL
JOY
FRGOVEEISSN
PEACE
r
y
b
b
y
r
is
JESUS
born!
fit in the words, then colour the star
colours: red yellow blue

Christmas Day (1/2) Christ is born

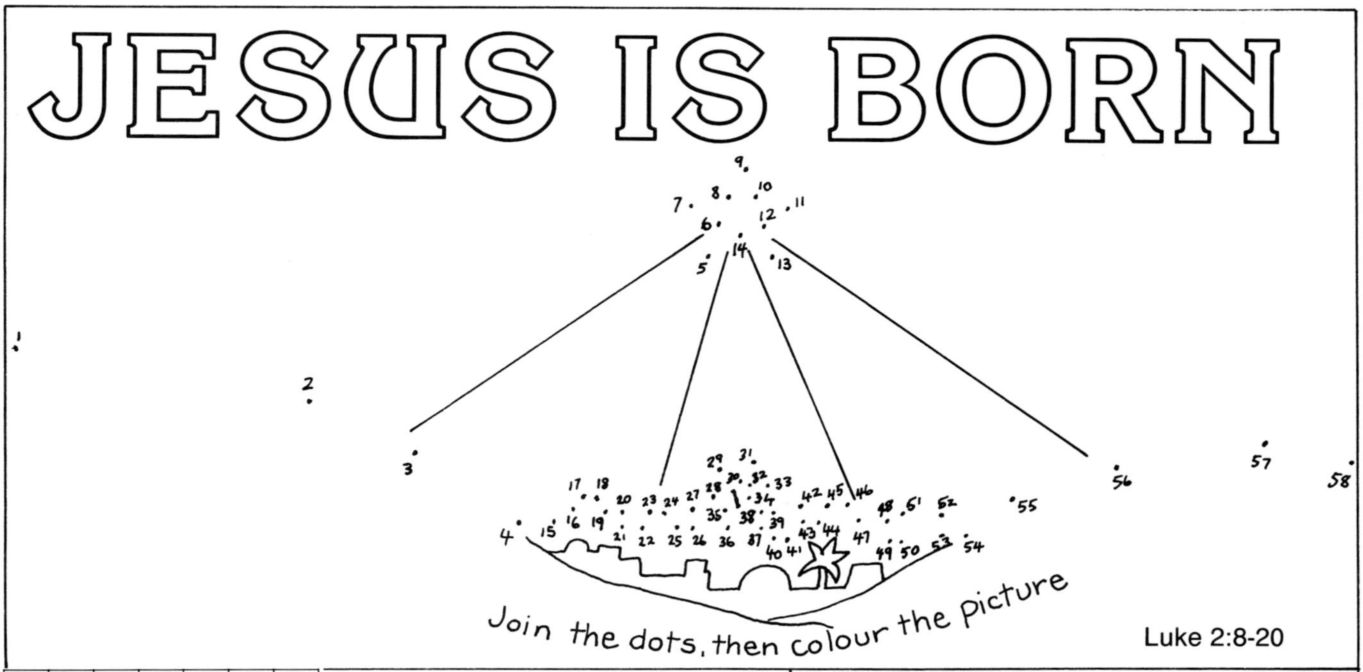

JESUS IS BORN
Join the dots, then colour the picture
Luke 2:8-20

G	L	O	R	Y	A	B
M	U	N	S	A	N	G
D	O	G	E	D	G	C
O	B	H	N	F	E	E
T	T	J	I	A	L	H
H	I	G	H	E	S	T

'GLORY TO GOD

IN THE HIGHEST'

SANG THE ANGELS

Who were the first people to be told the good news?

IE
+
N
+
OA
+
S

1st SUNDAY AFTER CHRISTMAS

Year 1 Theme: The Incarnation
Isaiah 7:10-14; Galatians 4:1-7; John 1:14-18

Discuss with the children what it means to be adopted. Some may have personal experience of being 'chosen' in this way into a family. They may have come across 'Cabbage Patch' dolls which come with an adoption certificate. There are often advertisements in local newspapers about children in care who are hoping to find a family willing to adopt them.

It is important that even young children have the opportunity to talk about such matters in a caring, sensitive atmosphere, and they are often touchingly aware of the importance of belonging to a family unit.

Now give the children lumps of modelling clay and ask them to make some kind of person-creature that they would like as a friend if it were alive. When the creatures are finished, display them and enjoy them.

Wouldn't it be wonderful if we really could bring them to life! Explain how God created beings whom he loved and actually brought to life, and see if they can guess the names of some of them. And not only did he give us life, he adopted us; so that makes us very, very special — we must be children in God's family. He is our parent who loves us enough to want us to eat, sleep, play, work, sing, laugh and cry in his company.

Write this notice to put with the models and bring the whole thing into church.

God made us, give us life,
and chose us as his children

God made us, gave us life,
and chose us as his children

Year 2 Theme: The Presentation
1 Samuel 1:20-end; Romans 12:1-8; Luke 2:22-40

Talk with the children about some of the things that have to be done when a baby is born, such as registering the child (show a birth certificate, and suggest they ask to see their own at home) and having a check-up with the doctor (put on a toy stethoscope) and preparing for the baby's baptism (show a christening robe or a picture of a baby being baptised).

Now tell them how, in the Law of Moses, whenever the first son was born, he was brought to the temple to be offered to God, together with a present of two doves or pigeons. (Show two paper ones.)

Using a doll, and four children to be Mary, Joseph, Simeon and Anna, tell today's Gospel reading with the children miming the actions. The other children should mime the parts of the people in the temple so no one is left out. Finally, help the children to make a pair of turtledoves each:

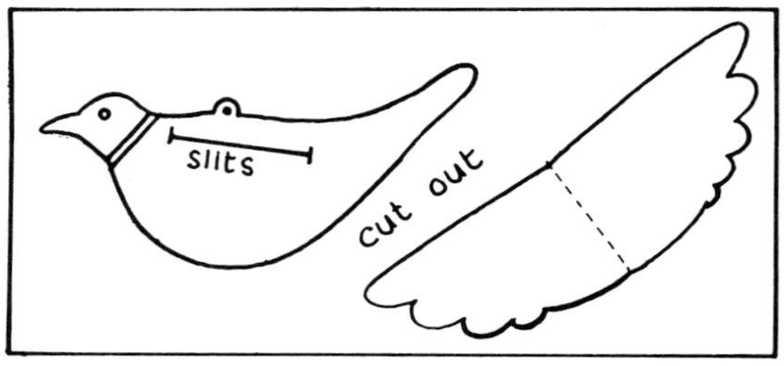
slits
cut out

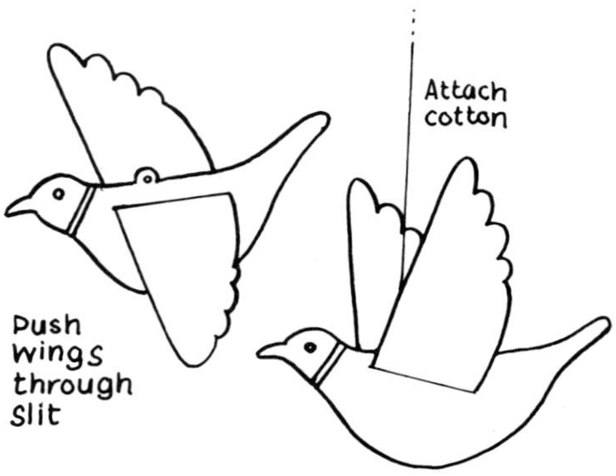
Attach cotton
Push wings through slit

Christmas 1 (1) The Incarnation

NO-ONE HAS EVER SEEN GOD . . .
THE SON HAS MADE HIM KNOWN.
John 1:14-18
God is
write them here
Which of these words are true of Jesus?
kind
loving
bad-tempered
stubborn
patient
loyal
grumpy
a cheat
honest
'ABBA' is a Hebrew word. Do you know what it means?
3 1 5 4 2 6
Key: A E F H T R
1 2 3 4 5 6

Christmas 1 (2) The Presentation

"JUST AS YOU PROMISED, MY EYES HAVE SEEN THE ONE WHO WILL SAVE US."
Luke 2:22-40
This man's name is
S M I O N E
He had hoped all his life to see the saviour of the world. And now......
THENIRECOGNISEDAJESUS
SWASHTHERESAVIOURS
Colour the dotted letters.
What are these birds for?
PAIR
LORD
SON
PIGEONS
SACRIFICE
Every first born --- was presented to the ----, and a --------- was offered, which was a ---- of turtle doves or -------.

2nd SUNDAY AFTER CHRISTMAS

Year 1 Theme: The Holy Family

Ecclesiasticus 3:2-7 or Exodus 12:21-27; Romans 8:11-17; Luke 2:41-end

Ask the children to share some of the funny or exciting things their family has done — an outing or holiday, perhaps; moving house or getting a pet — and together thank God for our families. If you have some family photographs, show the children a selection stretching across the generations (so they can see Grandma, perhaps, both as a child herself with her family, and also with her grandchildren in a recent picture). Talk about each person in a family being important and remembered, and link this with us all being part of another family as well: the family of God. He is our Father and we are all his children (even grandparents are children in God's family!) Just as we are special in our human families, so God our Father considers each one of us special.

Ask the children to draw all the members of their own families (extended family members and pets, too, if they wish) and help them to label everyone. Write under the picture 'God our Father, bless my family'. Try singing: *We belong to the family of God* (MWTP, 49).

Year 2 Theme: The Light of the World

Isaiah 60:1-6; Revelation 21:22-22:5; Matthew 2:1-12; 19-23

Prepare a cereal box 'television' and a strip of paper showing the night sky, the wise men on their journey, their visit to Herod, their adoration of Jesus and their departure by another route. Use these drawings as a guideline, or cut out pictures from Christmas cards and stick them on.

Tell the children the story of the wise men, rolling the pictures along as you do so; or ask two children to do the spoon twisting.

Talk about how we can all be like the star by shining brightly to lead people to Jesus. With their help, make a list of practical ways we can do this:

- stay close to Jesus
- get to know the Bible
- be kind and loving
- stand up for what is right
- let others know you're a Christian
- enjoy and care for God's world

Have six strips of card about 1 metre long and 5 cms wide, lay them down on the floor to make a star shape like this:

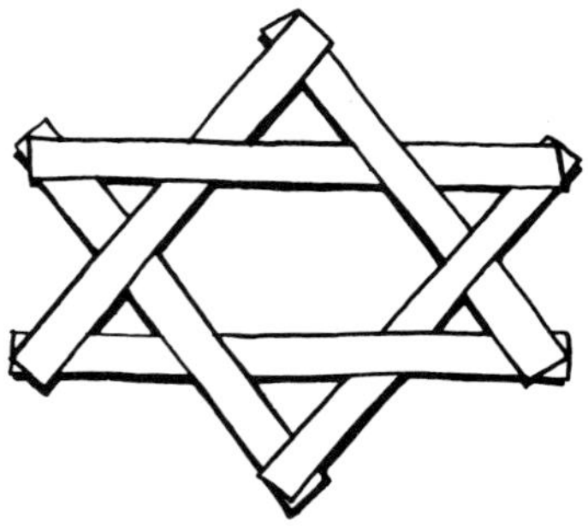

Write one of the six guidelines for being a star on each strip of card and let the children decorate them with tinsel and glue. Staple the strips together and carry the star into church, placing it near the altar, if possible.

stick firmly
stick firmly

WHEN JESUS WAS 12 YEARS OLD HE GOT LOST.

Luke 2:41-end

Help Mary and Joseph find Jesus

Have you ever been lost?
Draw a picture of it here.

Where did Mary and Joseph find Jesus in the end?

☐☐ ☐☐☐ ☐☐☐☐☐☐☐ ☐☐ ☐☐☐ ☐☐☐☐☐☐ ☐☐☐☐☐☐ ☐☐☐☐☐☐☐☐☐

HE THE IN WAS TEMPLE ASKING QUESTIONS SITTING

THEY FOLLOWED THE STAR AND FOUND JESUS.

Matthew 2:1-12, 19-23

BETHLEHEM
Which way did the star lead them?

A	G	D	E	D	O	R	E	H	F	L	B
W	W	O	L	L	O	F	I	R	X	Q	F
O	B	R	R	O	D	S	D	R	E	A	M
L	W	C	P	A	G	K	H	Y	C	O	E
L	M	V	J	Y	T	T	E	M	E	N	H
O	Z	F	P	I	H	S	R	O	W	N	L
F	R	A	N	K	I	N	C	E	N	S	E
D	A	U	B	W	D	G	I	K	S	Y	J

GOLD
FRANKINCENSE
MYRRH
WISE
MEN
FOLLOW
STAR
HEROD
DREAM
WORSHIP

THE EPIPHANY OF OUR LORD

Theme: The Wise Men come to Jesus

Years 1 and 2

Isaiah 49:1-6; Ephesians 3:1-12; Matthew 2:1-12

Tell or read the story of the wise men, with their gifts displayed on the table. (The Palm Tree version is called *Following a Star*.) If possible, have something of real gold, a thurible with incense burning, and some anointing oil. Talk about these things, and how we use them in our worship (or way of showing the "worth") of our God. How can we give God a present?

Wrap each child in Christmas wrapping paper and give each a label to write and decorate, thread on wool and hang round his neck. At the offering of gifts, let the 'presents' walk up to give themselves. The labels can be collected and blessed before they are returned to the children.

To dear God
with love
from
Elizabeth
xxx

The Epiphany of Our Lord (1/2) The Wise Men come to Jesus

WHERE IS HE WHO HAS BEEN BORN KING OF THE JEWS?
Matthew 2:1-12
Why was Herod worried about this?
might
He
was
new
afraid
that
take
a
king
his
power
What gifts can we bring to Jesus?
our RPIASE
our ITME
our OLEV
can you think of some others?

1st SUNDAY AFTER THE EPIPHANY

Theme: Revelation — The Baptism of Jesus

Year 1

1 Samuel 16:1-13a; Acts 10:34-38a; Matthew 3:13-end

If you have any pictures of the Jordan, show these first, so that the children realise that it is a real place and can identify more easily with events there.

Also have a large baking tray, some earth or sand, metal foil, stones and twigs, and plasticine. Explain that you are all going to make a model of the Jordan and then let the children help assemble it. With the foil make a trough which can be filled with water for the river. Plasticine models of people can also be made, one of whom is John, and one Jesus. The rest are the crowds. Make a dove too.

Then tell the story of Jesus' baptism, moving the models as you do so. Rattle a sheet of thick card as God's voice speaks.

Give the children cards to fill and colour, like this:

Jesus was baptised in the Jordan River
Rachel was baptised at

Year 2

Isaiah 42:1-7; Ephesians 2:1-10; John 1:29-34

Tell the children the story of John baptising Jesus, and show some pictures or slides of the river Jordan. (Your local Christian resource centre should have these to lend out).

Now help the children make these models, set in shoe boxes. They will need scissors, glue, colouring materials, cotton and sticky tape.

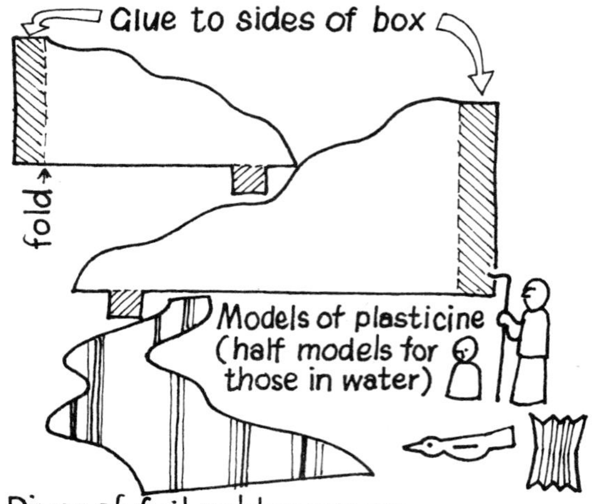
Glue to sides of box
fold
Models of plasticine (half models for those in water)
River of foil or blue paper

He is the chosen One of God!

'THIS IS MY SON, MY BELOVED.'

Matthew 3:13-end

(Read 1 Samuel 16:1-13)

Which of the sons of Jesse did Samuel anoint as king?

_ _ _ _ _

This is the advice God gave Samuel about which person to choose:

DON'T
BY A
JUDGE BY THE

Jesus was

by John in the river

'HE IS THE CHOSEN ONE OF GOD.'

Isaiah 42:1-7

Isaiah's Prophecy

My _ _ _ _ _ _ _ _ will not _ _ _ _ _ _ a bruised _ _ _ _ _ , or snuff out a smouldering _ _ _ _ _ . He will bring justice and light to all _ _ _ _ _ _ _ . He will open eyes that are _ _ _ _ _ _ and set captives _ _ _ _ .

people · wick · blind · servant · reed · free · break

Q. Why did John the Baptist duck people under the water?

A. As a

that their

were

away.

When Jesus was baptised, the Spirit came down on him from heaven. It looked like this.

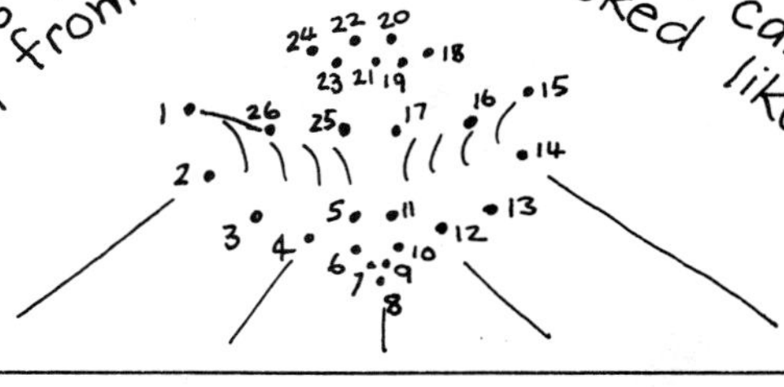

2nd SUNDAY AFTER THE EPIPHANY

Theme: Revelation — The First Disciples

Year 1

Jeremiah 1:4-10; Acts 26:1, 9-20; Mark 1:14-20

As the children come in, make a point of having various jobs that need doing. In each case say something like: 'Now, we need someone strong to move this table.'; 'We need two people to arrange these lovely flowers Matthew brought.' etc.

When everyone is ready, remind the children of these needs which various people offered to do. God also needs our help to do his work, and he is hoping we will offer our help so that he can use us to make the world a more loving, caring place. Lead the children in prayer —

Heavenly Father,
here I am —
please use me:
I would really like
to help you.

All of us here have been chosen and asked to help, just as the fishermen — Peter, Andrew, James and John — were chosen in Galilee. Tell or read today's Gospel and try singing the 'Follow me' song.

Have a fishing net (or net curtain) and ask each child to make a fish, using templates for the younger children. They write their own names on the fish and decorate them. Then they poke the fish into the net so the names show. Hang the net up in church, putting a notice beside it saying: 'I will make you fishers of men'

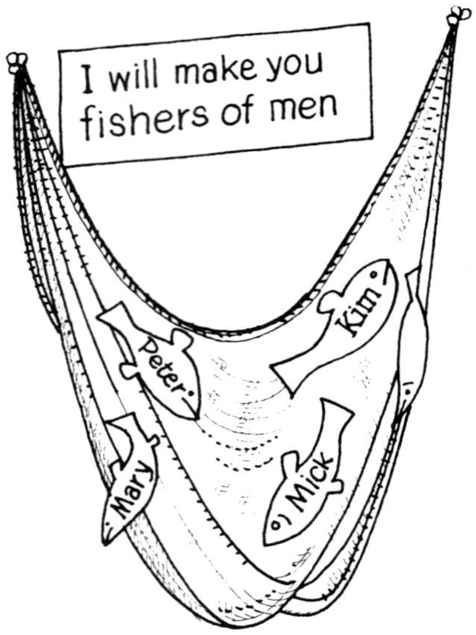
I will make you fishers of men
Peter
Kim
Mary
Mick

Year 2

1 Samuel 3:1-10; Galatians 1:11-end; John 1:35-end

Tell the children the story of God calling to Samuel, involving two of them in the story to mime the events.

Now divide them into two groups to play a game. The children in one line are given a different short message which they have to shout across to their partner on the far side of the room. The trouble is that everyone will shout their message at the same time! See how long it takes before everyone has received the right message. Then gather everyone round in a circle and hold up a pin. Try to hear the pin drop. Once this stillness has been achieved, talk quietly with them about the need to be quiet and still in our prayer if we are to know what God wants us to do.

Finish with a time of prayer based on the sounds we can hear when we close our eyes and really listen. Pray for travellers and drivers when you hear traffic; for those with colds and others who are ill; for babies and those being born; thank God for the wind or the rain, and so on. Encourage the children to add their prayers; there is no better way to learn to pray than by praying.

COME AND FOLLOW ME!

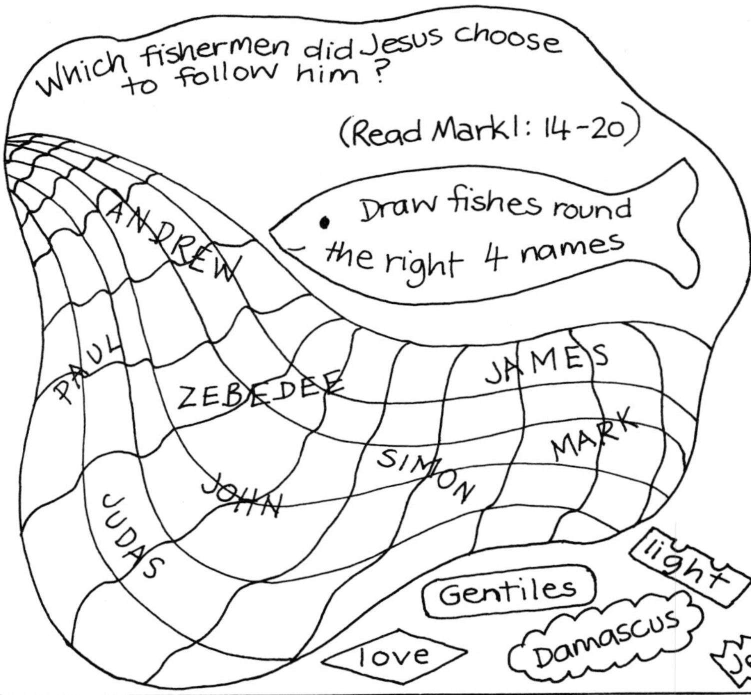
Which fishermen did Jesus choose to follow him?
(Read Mark 1: 14-20)
Draw fishes round the right 4 names
ANDREW
PAUL
ZEBEDEE
JAMES
SIMON
MARK
JOHN
JUDAS

Saul! Saul! Why are you persecuting me?

Paul was on his way to ______ to persecute the ______ of ______ when ______ spoke to him in a blinding ______ and called him to tell the ______ the good news of God's ______.

light Gentiles Damascus love Jesus followers

Acts 26:1, 9-20

HERE I AM, LORD!

1 Samuel 3:1-10

S	A	M	U	E	L	B	C	A
G	D	I	K	E	I	C	T	N
O	P	E	E	L	S	A	S	S
D	H	R	F	M	T	L	E	W
N	H	E	L	E	E	L	I	E
T	O	G	M	J	N	I	R	R
S	R	P	T	A	I	N	P	E
U	L	V	Q	C	N	G	P	D
E	C	I	O	V	G	W	D	Y

SAMUEL was ASLEEP in the TEMPLE when he heard someone CALLING his NAME. He thought it was ELI the PRIEST. THREE times the VOICE came, so Eli realised that GOD was calling Samuel. Next time God called, Samuel ANSWERED, 'Speak, Lord, I am LISTENING.'

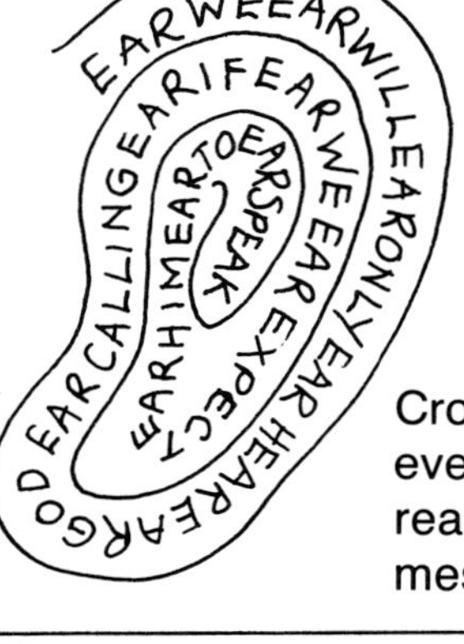
EARWEEARWILLEARONLYEARHEAREARGODEARCALLINGEARIFEARWEEAREXPECTEARHIMEARTOEARSPEAK

Cross out every EAR to read the message!

Hello Nathanael!
How does he know me?
John 1: 35-end
Colour the picture

3rd SUNDAY AFTER THE EPIPHANY

Theme: Revelation — Signs of Glory

Year 1

Exodus 33:12-end; 1 John 1:1-7; John 2:1-11

Display some posters of vineyards — travel agents should be able to supply some pictures — and have a cluster of grapes on the table (seedless are best for young children). Share the grapes out, and talk about how the juice is squeezed out and mellowed carefully in vats before being bottled and drunk, perhaps on a special happy occasion like weddings, or, in some countries, with everyday meals.

Read or tell them about the wedding in Cana when the wine ran out, and Jesus gave them wine from water.

When have they seen wine used in church? Talk about the celebration which we share there — Jesus shares his life with us.

Help the children make a card like this:

Drink this, all of you
My blood takes away your sins and gives you
LIFE

Year 2

Deuteronomy 8:1-6; Philippians 4:10-20; John 6:1-14

Cut out from card five small rolls and two fish, colour them and put them in a lunch box, and use this as you tell the children today's Gospel. It will help them imagine it all better if you enlist their help in being the crowd walking round the lake, listening to Jesus' words, one boy being Philip and another the one who had a lunch box which he offered and so on.

Then help them make five barley loaves and two fish each, using the card ones and templates. On the back of each item write a word which can be shuffled into a prayer, like this:

Look
Jesus
here
I
am
Use
me

WATER INTO WINE!

John 2:1-11

Moses asked God to show him his glory. How did God show him?

He put ----- in a cleft of the -----, and shielded him with his ----- while his glory ------- by. Then he ---- his hand ---- so that Moses saw his ----.

back hand Moses rock passed away took

Exodus 33:18-23

Jesus showed his glory by the signs he did

Where? + a
C
W
What?
IN
2
W
W
Why? t y
d
OUT
T

JESUS FEEDS 5000 PEOPLE.

John 6:1-14

Draw in the faces, then colour the picture.

START
find your way to the bread and fish

Jesus showed his glory by this

Colour the dotted letters.

4th SUNDAY AFTER THE EPIPHANY

Theme: Revelation — The New Temple

Year 1

1 Kings 8:22-30; 1 Corinthians 3:10-17; John 2:13-22

Bring along a household repair manual which has clear diagrams in it, a piece of sandpaper for each child and an assortment of wood offcuts or driftwood, and plenty of varnish.

First show the children how important it is to prepare a wall before you paint it — otherwise the paint will not last. Show them how cracks need to be cleaned out before they can be filled and wood sanded down before it is varnished. Explain how repentance is the necessary cleaning out and preparation before any growing can start in our Christian lives. This is made clearer if you have a chart with diagrams similar to the repair manual like this:

Give the children a chart to use in prayer during the week, which helps them review areas in their lives which need to be sanded down or cleaned up for Christ to make beautiful and useful.

Now let the children select a piece of wood and sand it down smoothly before varnishing it. It may be used as an ornament, or a paper weight.

How to build a new life in Christ
1 Inspect the damage
Wasting time
wanting my own way
Telling lies
Pride
Unkindness
Being mean
Greed
2 Tell God you are sorry and want him to help you put things right
Christ
3. Enjoy building. Let God work through you

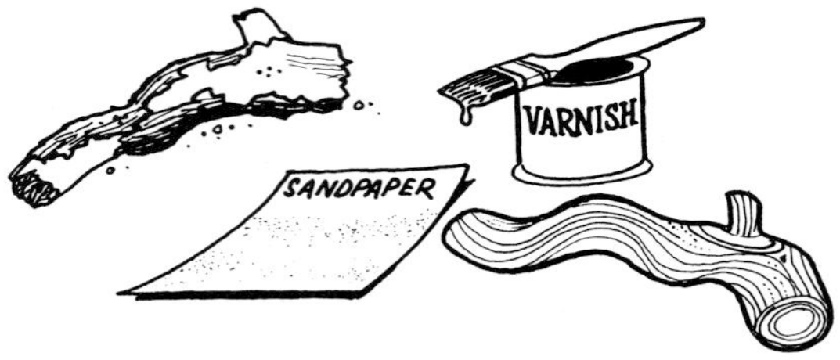
VARNISH
SANDPAPER

Year 2

Jeremiah 7:1-11; Hebrews 12:18-end; John 4:19-26

Talk about being honest with God: saying our prayers and then being unkind, lazy or boastful, for instance. Explain that this is really lying, and we need to make it up with Jesus by saying we are sorry and having him forgive us — which he ALWAYS will. Have a short prayer time to do this.

Tell the children how God makes our lives beautiful and then builds us into his living church. Give each child an ordinary-looking muddy stone. Have ready several bowls of soapy water and kitchen roll, with protective aprons and scrubbing brushes. The children clean and decorate their stones and then arrange them on an outline of a cross. Nightlights can be placed among the stones. Gather round this cross to sing to Jesus some praise songs.

YOU ARE GOD'S TEMPLE WHERE GOD'S SPIRIT LIVES.

1 Corinthians 3:16

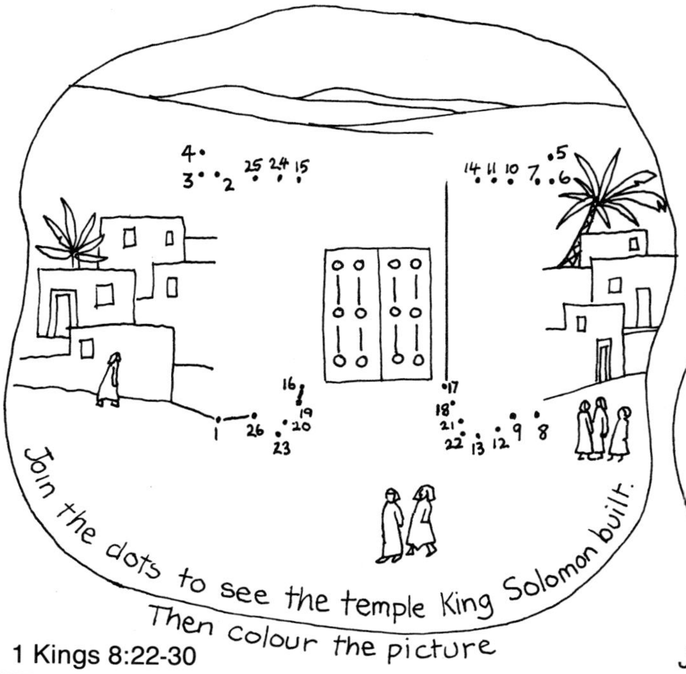
Join the dots to see the temple King Solomon built.
Then colour the picture

1 Kings 8:22-30

What did Jesus find in the temple?
S _ _ _ _ _
H E S E P
P _ _ _ _ _ _
P G O I N S E
M _ _ _ _ _
N O E Y M
C _ _ _ _ _ _
A T C E T L E

John 2:13-16

WE MUST WORSHIP GOD IN SPIRIT AND TRUTH.

John 4:19-26

Why isn't God pleased with their worship?
The Sabbath day
Monday, Tuesday, Wednesday, Thursday....
Jeremiah 7:3-11

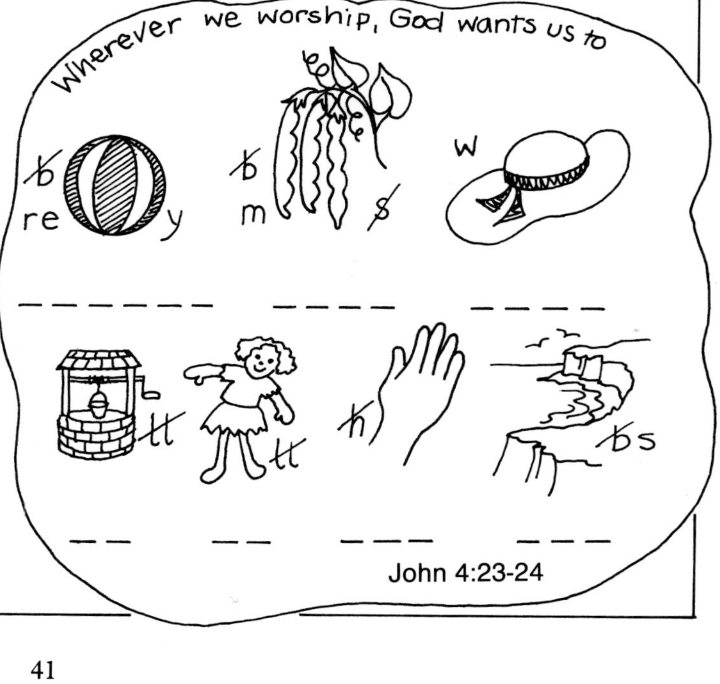
Wherever we worship, God wants us to
re y
m
W
John 4:23-24

5th SUNDAY AFTER THE EPIPHANY

Theme: Revelation — The Wisdom of God

Year 1

Proverbs 2:1-9 or Ecclesiasticus 42:15-end; 1 Corinthians 3:18-end; Matthew 12:38-42

Bring along a toy owl, or a picture of an owl, and talk with the children about what we think of as being wise. It's not so much knowing a lot of facts as knowing how to act in the best way whenever you're faced with a problem. Some of them may know the Brownies' story of the wise owl, and there are lots of fairy stories showing wise people solving problems in very practical and effective ways.

Now, using a selection of pictures and objects — whatever you have available — talk with them about the ways in which our God is wise. Explore such areas as animal camouflage, the growth of food, seasons, gravity, electricity and the balance of nature. Jesus showed that he was wise in the way he loved and understood people, and the more loving we are the wiser we shall become, even if some people think we are fools.

Help the children to make a collage of their own and cut-out pictures showing the glory of God in our world. Call the collage:

'the work of the Lord is full of his glory'

The work of the Lord is full of his glory

Epiphany 5 (1/2) Revelation — The Wisdom of God

THE WORK OF THE LORD
IS FULL OF HIS GLORY
Ecclesiasticus 42:16
What does God's world tell us about God? He must be:
careful
wise
mean
powerful
loving
selfish
dull
imaginative
circle the right words

6th SUNDAY AFTER THE EPIPHANY

Theme: Revelation — Parables

Years 1 and 2

2 Samuel 12:1-10; Romans 1:18-25; Matthew 13:24-30

The Palm Tree Bible Stories series has a very readable version of this story, which could be told to the children first. It is called *Evil Beezel's Wicked Trick*.

Talk about what things they think are like the weeds, and which the wheat, and how sensible God is not to risk damaging the crop by pulling up the weeds before the wheat is strong enough. Then divide them so that some draw and cut out wheat and some thorny weeds. Stick them all on to a poster, on which is written: 'Let them both grow till the harvest'.

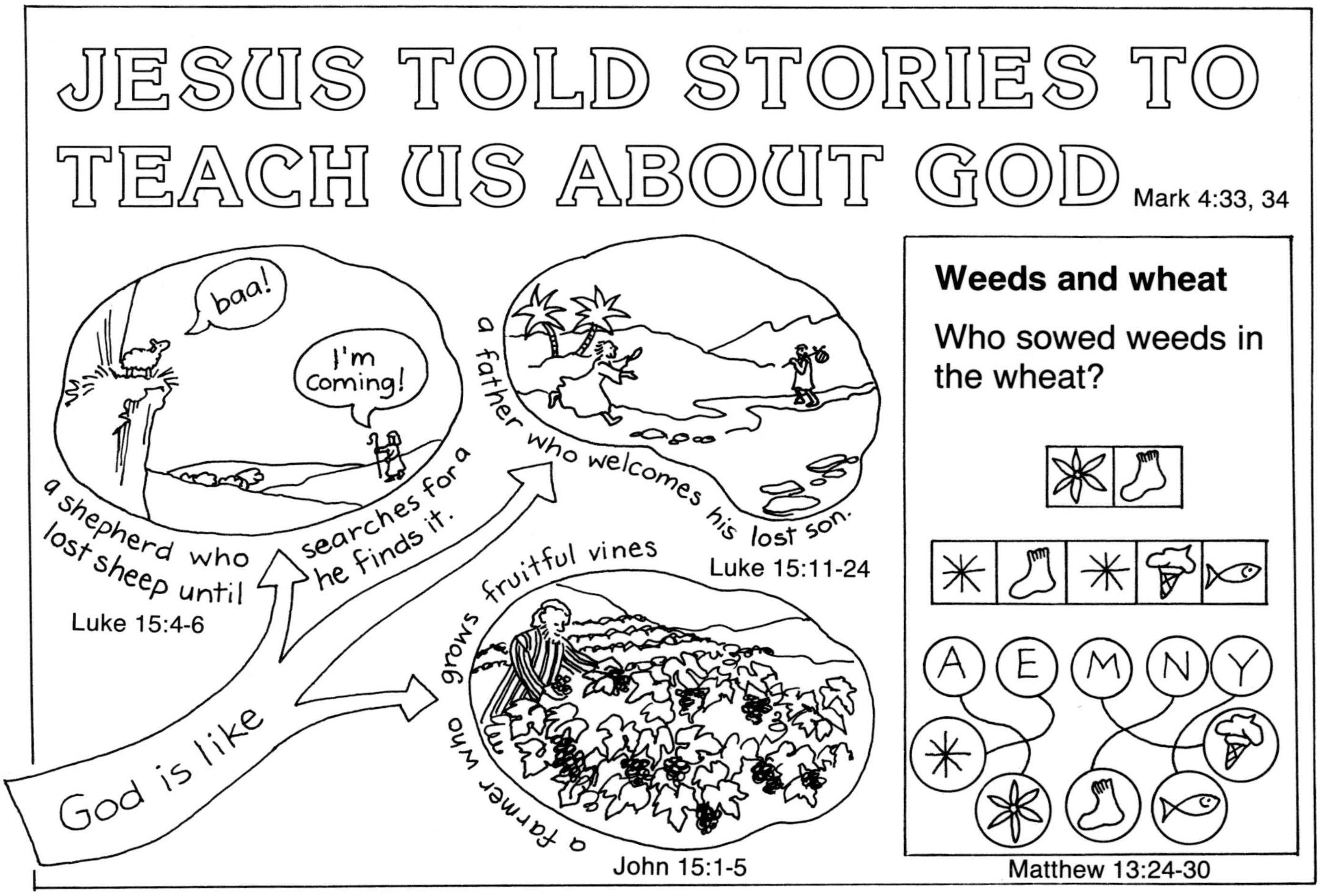

JESUS TOLD STORIES TO TEACH US ABOUT GOD
Mark 4:33, 34
baa!
I'm coming!
a shepherd who lost sheep until
searches for a he finds it.
Luke 15:4-6
a father who welcomes his lost son.
Luke 15:11-24
a farmer who grows fruitful vines
John 15:1-5
God is like
Weeds and wheat
Who sowed weeds in the wheat?
A
E
M
N
Y
Matthew 13:24-30

9th SUNDAY BEFORE EASTER

Theme: Christ the Teacher

Year 1

Isaiah 30:18-21; 1 Corinthians 4:8-13; Matthew 5:1-12

Bring along an assortment of advertisements mounted on a board so the children can see them as they come in. You could have some on tape as well from television and radio.

Why do firms advertise? So as to get us to buy their product. Every day we are encouraged to WANT and to GET. The more we GET, the more we WANT. Stick a thin strip of paper over the advertisements which says: GET, GET, GET. WANT, WANT, WANT. GET, GET, GET all across it.

SALE
BUY NOW
GET GET GET GET GET GET
WANT WANT WANT WANT
SALE

But if *things* are most important in our life, they make life harder, not happier. Have some heavy chains, stone-filled bags with straps etc. with labels on such as:

— I wish I could have...
— If only I could...
— I want...
— Leave that alone — it's MINE.

One by one, hang them around yourself or a child who volunteers, until he is really loaded down.

Jesus says to us: 'Trust in me, instead of in THINGS. You'll find you're much happier.' Then unload your volunteer and pin on him an 'I'm for Jesus' badge. Now he is less cluttered, able to move and run about (let him demonstrate).

When we trust in Jesus we can enjoy what we are given, but also enjoy giving away. We can enjoy owning, but also enjoy sharing. We can be happy when we have lots of toys, but also be happy when we haven't got many.

Let the children make an 'I'm for Jesus' badge to wear, and ask them to try giving instead of getting at least once each day this week.

I'm for Jesus

Year 2

Proverbs 3:1-8; 1 Corinthians 2:1-10; Luke 8:4b-15

Have some grain (pearl barley will do, if no wheat is available) and a baking tray arranged with the varied surfaces on it like this:

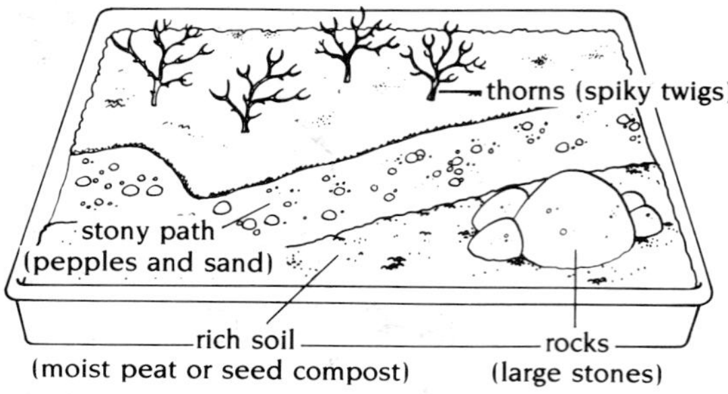
thorns (spiky twigs)
stony path
(pepples and sand)
rich soil
(moist peat or seed compost)
rocks
(large stones)

As you tell the story, sprinkle the seed so that some falls on each section. Talk about which will not grow and which will do the best. You could have some fresh plants to press into the good soil to emphasise the point.

Now explain how Jesus used this story to tell us about how people react to God's good news. See if they can work out what some of the images mean. Then help the children to write captions for each section, stick them on lolly sticks and push them into the model. Others can decorate the background and title. The whole model will then look something like this:

A sower once went out to sow...

Bring the model into church and display it where the rest of the congregation can see it as they come to receive Communion.

JESUS SHOWS US WHAT GOD IS LIKE.

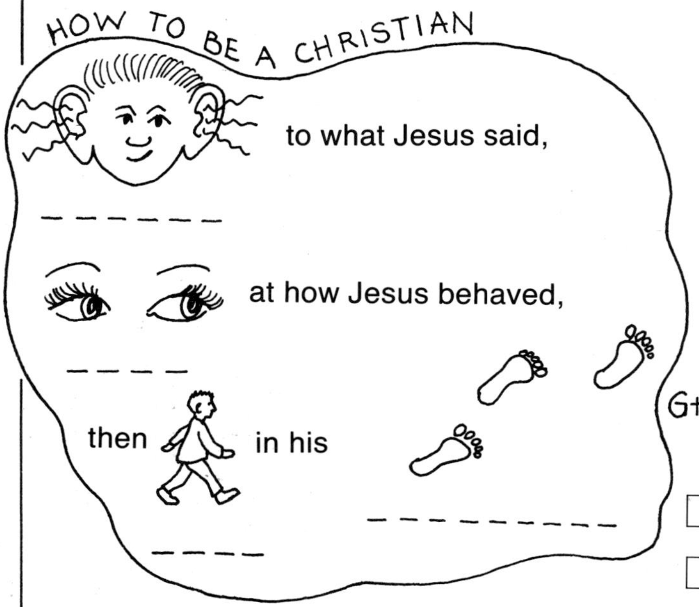
HOW TO BE A CHRISTIAN
to what Jesus said,
at how Jesus behaved,
then
in his

Try this sum:

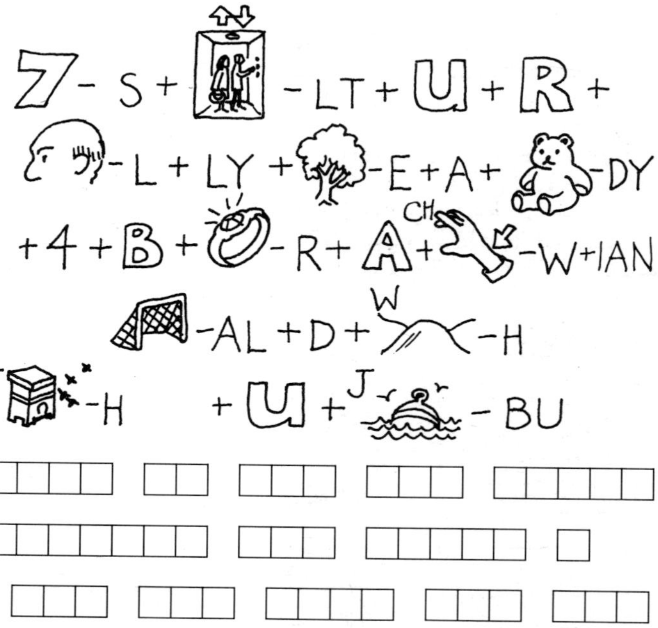
7 - S +
- LT + U + R +
- L + LY +
- E + A +
- DY
+ 4 + B +
- R + A + CH
- W + IAN
- AL + D + W
- H
G +
- H
+ U + J
- BU

Matthew 5:1-12

SOME SEED FELL INTO GOOD SOIL AND GREW.

What will these seeds grow into?

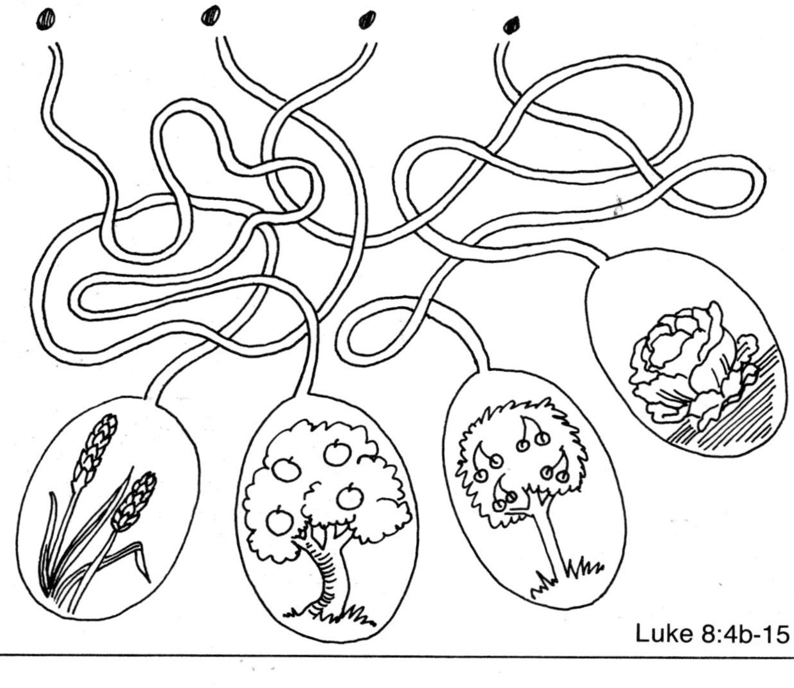

A	C	F	I	O	K	G	R	S	V
F	A	R	M	E	R	A	M	E	T
B	O	B	U	E	E	I	D	E	L
N	I	H	W	P	H	T	Z	D	N
Y	S	R	P	H	T	A	P	E	F
L	G	S	D	J	I	H	V	K	U
E	K	E	B	S	W	L	I	O	S
K	C	W	Y	J	Q	C	W	H	G
R	O	T	I	U	R	F	M	C	Q
S	R	D	T	H	O	R	N	S	X

FARMER	WITHER	BIRDS
SOW	THORNS	GREW
SEED	CHOKED	ROCK
PATH	SOIL	FRUIT

Luke 8:4b-15

8th SUNDAY BEFORE EASTER

Theme: Christ the Healer

Year 1

Zephaniah 3:14-end; James 5:13-16a; Mark 2:1-12

Tell today's story of the paralytic who was let down through the roof, using a simple model which the children make first. One group makes a house from a white shoe box. At this stage do not mention the way the man's friend got him to Jesus; just talk about the typical design of such a house with outside steps to a flat roof in which there was often an opening.

Other children make a stretcher-bed with a paralysed man on it, and others make a large crowd of people. Arrange the model on sand-coloured paper and put a few model donkeys and chickens around, and a palm tree or two.

Place Jesus and his friends in the house first, and add other visitors as you explain how word got around that Jesus could heal the sick. When the men arrive with their paralysed friend the children will see that they can't get to Jesus. Ask what they might do now. Give up? Seeing the problem will help them appreciate the men's faith and their determination and persistence. They may even suggest using the hole in the roof.

All through the story help them to identify with the different characters so that they can, in some sense, become 'eye witnesses' to the events.

Year 2

2 Kings 5:1-14; 2 Corinthians 12:1-10; Mark 7:24-end

Palm Tree have a version of Naaman's story of healing, called *Naaman's Spots*. Read this, or another version with pictures, and then go through the story again with the children acting it out. A narrator holds everything together, and children not involved as main characters are servants and interested onlookers.

Children are often very good at praying for others, and are helped by pictures. Explain to them how important their prayers are in making people better, and help them make a praying scrap book. On the first page they stick a picture of Jesus healing someone, and on the others they will be drawing, or sticking in pictures and photographs of any prayer needs for healing. These may be from newspapers and magazines, snapshots etc. Encourage the children to use their books regularly, and from time to time give them the name or picture of others who need their prayers. This becomes beneficial in both directions — the elderly, sick or lonely in the parish gain great support from knowing the child is praying for them, and the child is learning unselfish prayer and a deeper friendship with Jesus.

My Praying Book

STAND UP, TAKE YOUR BED AND WALK!

Colour the picture. Mark 2:1-12

What did Jesus say to the man before he healed his body?

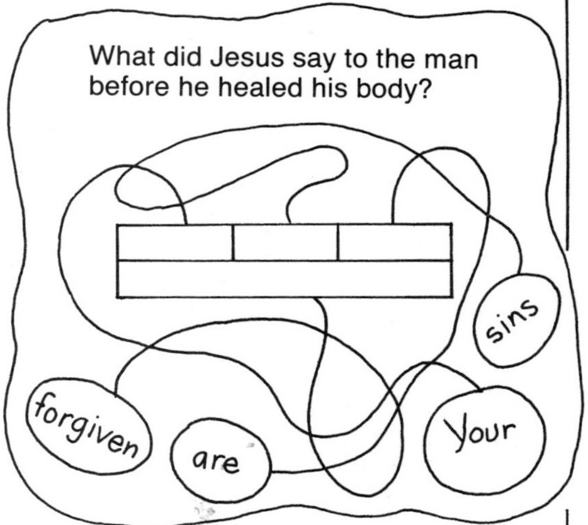
sins
forgiven
are
your

What did the man's friends have lots of?

Colour the dotted letters.

HE EVEN MAKES THE DEAF HEAR AND THE DUMB SPEAK!

Mark 7:31-37

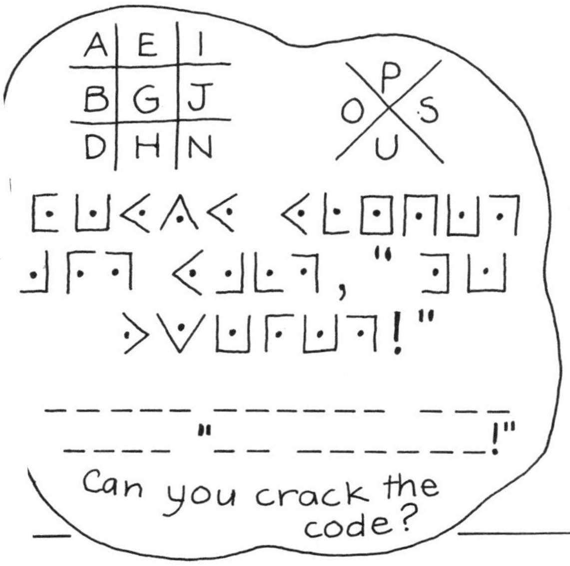
A E I
B G J
D H N
P O S U
Can you crack the code?

★ How did the deaf man get to Jesus?
(Cross out every BRING)
BRINGHIBRINGSBRINGFRIBRINGENDSBRING
BROUBRINGGHTBRINGHIMBRINGALBRINGONG.

★ Why did they bother?
(Cross out every FAITH)
THE FAITHYFAITHTRUSFAITHTEDFAITHTHAT
JEFAITHSUSFAITHWOFAITHULDFAITHHEFAITHLP.

7th SUNDAY BEFORE EASTER

Theme: Christ the Friend of Sinners

Year 1

Hosea 14:1-7; Philemon 1-16; Mark 2:13-17

Tell the children the story of today's Gospel as a narrator of a play. Arrange the chairs as an audience and set up one end of the room to be the 'stage'. If there is a screen, or space for a background picture of hills, so much the better. Give the children their parts in advance, but they can sit as audience until needed.

As the characters are mentioned, another helper discreetly tells them to move to the stage, and they act out what the narrator is saying. You may find they join in and speak their own words. If not, they can either use the narrator's words or mime. Speak slowly and clearly, and give enough time for the children to act their parts at each stage of the story. Here is a possible 'script':

On stage: Matthew, sitting at money table, a beggar, two women buying cloth from a man, one man paying his taxes, and Jesus.

One day Jesus was walking slowly through a town, chatting to the people. He saw a man called Matthew sitting collecting money from the Romans. Jonah was poor and told Matthew he couldn't afford to pay today.

Jonah: I can't afford to pay you today.

Matthew shook his fist at Jonah angrily. He told him he had to pay or he would put him in prison.

Matthew: You'll *have* to pay. If you don't, I'll put you in prison.

The man went away sadly. Just then Jesus came up to Matthew and shook hands with him. The other people were surprised to see a good man like Jesus talking to a bad man like Matthew. They told their friends about it.

One of the women to audience: You know that good man, Jesus? Well, he's being friendly with that tax-collector, Matthew! It doesn't seem right to me.

Then Jesus told Matthew he wanted him as one of his followers, one of his special friends.

Jesus: Come and follow me, Matthew.

Matthew was very happy that Jesus had chosen him. He was quite surprised, too. He jumped up straight away and told Jesus he would love to follow him.

Matthew: Yes, Jesus, I'll come. I'd love to follow you!

He even invited Jesus to dinner that day.

Matthew: Will you come to dinner with me today?

Jesus thanked him and said that he would love to come.

Jesus: Thank you, Matthew. I'd love to come.

So together they went off to Matthew's house. On their way home, Matthew kept inviting his friends to join in the dinner party.

General conversation: Would you like to come to dinner? — Yes please; thank you etc.

Till by the time they reached Matthew's house there was quite a crowd. Matthew showed them all where to sit down, and gave Jesus the seat at the head of the table. Then they all had a lovely feast with lots to eat and drink. There were quite a lot of bad people among the guests, but Jesus was quite happy to be with them. A church leader came and looked at Jesus eating with all the sinners. He asked Jesus why he was with people like that. Didn't he know what kind of people they were?

Pharisee: Why are you mixing with these sinners, Jesus? Don't you know what they're like?

Jesus came over to him. He explained that God loves people whatever they're like, so we must be forgiving as well.

Jesus: God loves people whatever they are like, you see. So if God is ready to forgive, we must forgive too.

He said it was like a doctor — he does not visit the healthy ones, he visits those who are ill.

Jesus: I'll try and explain. A doctor doesn't come to see the healthy people, does he? He comes to help those who are ill. And God comes to put us right, when we go wrong.

And Jesus went back to eat dinner with all the sinners who needed his love to heal them.

Year 2

Numbers 15:32-36; Colossians 1:18-23; John 8:2-11

Have a blackboard, coloured chalk, and an effective board rubber. Have an old dirty sack or bag labelled SINS in nasty looking letters. Inside have separate cards — jagged and irregular, on which are written:

- telling lies;
- stealing;
- pushing someone over;
- spoiling someone's toys;

etc.

Ask one child to scatter them all around, and each picks one up. Each is written on the blackboard.

Explain how Jesus can wipe them right out, if we are really sorry. (Now rub them out.) How do we show we are sorry?

Let the children draw a beautiful picture on the blackboard for Jesus, and bring it into church.

Jesus came to save sinners!

Mark 2:13-17

Whenever we are sorry for what we do wrong, Jesus will

Q Why were the Pharisees complaining?

A a) Because Jesus ate too much at the party
b) Because Jesus came from Nazareth
c) Because Jesus was friends with bad people
d) Because Jesus pretended to be a doctor

See Mark 2:13-17

4
m
2
f
+t

Jesus Christ is the friend of sinners

Colossians 1:18-23

1 God
2 knows
3 this
4 and
5 he
6 still
7 loves
8 us
9 !

Jigsaw Message
1 Find the shape that fits
2 Write in the word on the person
very
find
what
is
it
do
to
difficult
and
right
all
we
good

1st SUNDAY IN LENT

Theme: The King and the Kingdom: Temptation

Year 1

Genesis 2:7-9; 3:1-7; Hebrews 2:14-end; Matthew 4:1-11

Tell the children the story of Adam and Eve explaining that it was their disobedience which cut them off from the happy life they had before with God. Then help them make a large collage picture of the garden with the tree of knowledge in the middle. Make sure all the other trees have lovely fruit as well as this one; there was, after all, no actual need for them to eat its fruit. Use lots of bright materials, or colours cut from magazine pages, and write on the picture 'Adam and Eve did not do as God told them. That spoilt things.'

Then give them two large twigs each and make them into a simple cross. This is another tree of life. Help them to see how Jesus did obey, even though it meant he was killed. Because he obeyed, he put everything right again. So now, if we do wrong, we can be completely forgiven, all because of Jesus.

Use a prayer of penitence and thanks for forgiveness.

Heavenly Father,
we are very sorry
that we have hurt you
and each other
and spoilt your world.
Thank you for sending Jesus
to put things right.
Please forgive us
because of his goodness. Amen

Year 2

Genesis 4:1-10; Hebrews 4:12-end; Luke 4:1-13

TEMPTATIONS
BE SELFISH!
TAKE THE EASY WAY OUT!
SHOW OFF!
JESUS SAID
No I'll do it God's way - the hard, good way of love!

Try to show that the easy ways are not always the best or most effective ways of doing something.

a. Have two pictures of bread. One teacher tears one picture out ('I need to stick it on a poster and tearing is quicker'). The other cuts it carefully ('It took longer but it was much better').
b. Nana's birthday. Two brothers — one makes a card himself, the other asks Mum to buy him one. It may be very smart, and the homemade one may be a bit gluey, but which shows most love? Jesus was tempted three times:

'Use your power
to make bread' —
be selfish;

'I'll give you the world so long
as you worship ME' —
take the easy way out;

'Jump off the temple to
show them your power' —
show off.

Instead, Jesus said 'No, I'll do it God's way — the hard, good way of love.'

Lent 1 (1) The King and the Kingdom: Temptation

JESUS WAS TEMPTED AS WE ARE.

Matthew 4:1-2

Jesus fasting in the desert

Adam ___ Eve
were tempted
God. Afterwards
they felt

Genesis 3:1-7

M	B	D	A	E	R	B
A	A	L	O	N	E	Y
K	T	N	E	L	O	G
E	S	E	H	T	F	E
S	T	O	N	E	S	V
T	R	I	D	Y	M	I
C	A	N	N	O	T	L

'MAKE THESE STONES INTO BREAD.'

'MAN CANNOT LIVE BY BREAD ALONE.'

('BREAD' is shown only once in the grid.)

Lent 1 (2) The King and the Kingdom: Temptation

IF YOU ARE THE SON OF GOD . . .

Luke 4:1-13

What happened in the wilderness?
Jesus was
his
in the

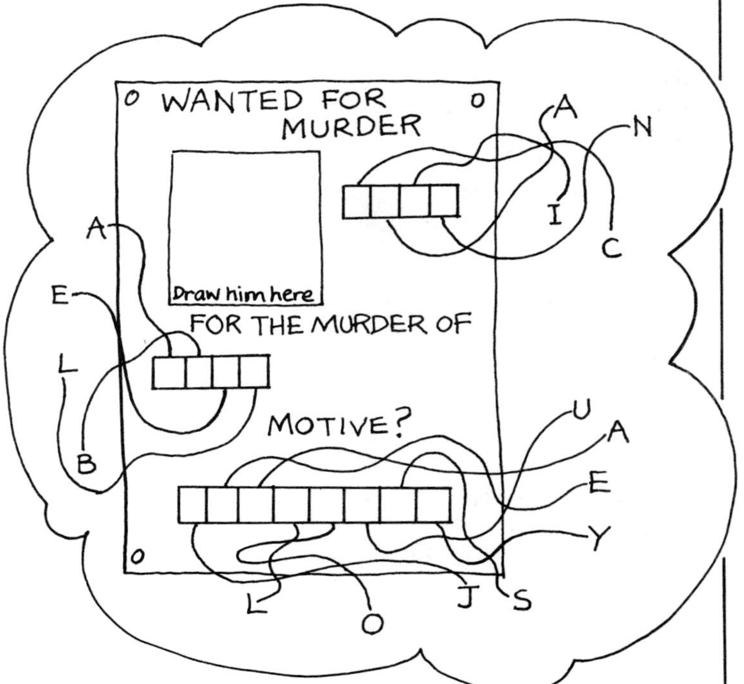

WANTED FOR MURDER
Draw him here
FOR THE MURDER OF
MOTIVE?

Genesis 4:1-10

2nd SUNDAY IN LENT

Theme: The King and the Kingdom — Conflict

Year 1

Genesis 6:11-end; 1 John 4:1-6; Luke 19:41-end

Show the children some pictures from traditional stories where it is very obvious who is the good character and who is the bad one. You could have a thumbs up sign whenever you point to a 'goodie' and a hiss whenever the 'baddie' appears. Then talk with them about how much harder it often is in real life to decide what is good and what is evil. Think, for instance, of when you make yourself late for school (hiss for bad) because you stopped to help at a bicycle accident (thumbs up for good), or when you offer to carry the shopping (thumbs up) so Dad won't notice a bar of chocolate you have stolen (hiss).

So how can we know for certain what is right and wrong? If you have the recording of Pinnochio, play and sing along with Jimminy Cricket, the voice of conscience. Through our conscience, God shows us which way is right, but we have to listen hard, or we may not hear. When we pray about a problem, Jesus will guide us through it safely. That's what Noah did, and he and his family were brought safely through the flood.

Help the children make this ark to remind them.

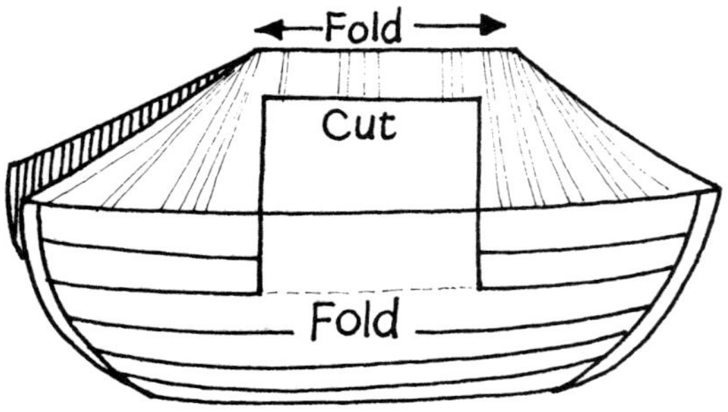
Fold
Cut
Fold

Year 2

Genesis 7:17-end; 1 John 3:1-10; Matthew 12:22-32

Start with a game of Simon Says. Then spread out a number of cards on which are written bits of advice or an order. Some are encouraging selfishness and greed — such as 'You bought those sweets; why give any away?' or 'Don't bother to clear up'. Others reflect the life and teaching of Jesus — such as 'Surprise Nana and Grandad with a letter' or 'Give Dad a hand with the washing up'. Together, sort out which things are what Jesus says, and try to put the Jesus Says game into practice in our lives.

Now tell them about Noah, who did this very well. Read or tell them the story — Palm Tree's version is called *Noah's Big Boat*. Work together on a large picture of the sea raging, and Noah's ark safely floating about on it.

Lent 2 (1) The King and the Kingdom: Conflict

GOD SAW THE WHOLE WORLD...

It is not easy to stand up for what is right, but whenever we do, God gives us

CAOTURYAPGEL

and

THAEMLOPE

Colour the dotted letters.

PAIR THE ANIMALS TO READ THE MESSAGE

Noah
saved
he
on
God's
because
was
way
went
living

WAS CORRUPT

Genesis 6:11-end

Lent 2 (2) The King and the Kingdom: Conflict

1 John 3:1-10

THOSE ON GOD'S SIDE ARE THOSE WHO DO WHAT IS RIGHT.

NOAH WAS ON GOD'S SIDE

Genesis 7:17-end

KEY:

A	D	F	G	H	I	N	O	P	R
14	13	12	11	10	9	8	7	6	5

S	T	U	W
4	3	2	1

CRACK THE CODE TO READ THE MESSAGE

11,7,12 1,14,8,3,4 2,4 3,7

4,3,14,8,13 2,6 13,7,5 1,10,14,3

9,4 5,9,11,10,3 14,8,13 11,7,7,13

3rd SUNDAY IN LENT

Theme: The King and the Kingdom — Suffering

Year 1

Genesis 22:1-13; Colossians 1:24-end; Luke 9:18-27

This is a particularly difficult theme for children to tackle, but if presented in a sensitive way it provides rich ground for teaching.

Beforehand prepare a duplicated sheet of A4 paper so that when folded it shows Abraham's offering on one side and God's on the other. Give them out and help the children fold them into zigzag books. Then read them through, looking at the pictures and adding details as you go. Help them to see why Abraham had already made his offering without actually doing anything to hurt Isaac. Are they ever asked to give anything up? Sharing toys willingly is offering God a sacrifice. So is giving up viewing time to help at home; offering someone your favourite sweet; sticking up for someone even if you get laughed at; being friendly when you feel like being thoroughly grumpy.

God's promise to Abraham would come true through his son, Isaac
ABRAHAM! I will make you the father of a whole nation- my chosen people shall be your grandchildren and great-grand-children
ABRAHAM! I want you to give up Isaac as an offering to me
Isaac? But he's my son- I love him
Very well Lord. I trust you with my son
Abraham had given his offering already - by being willing to give up something he loved
STOP, ABRAHAM! Now I know you really trust me. Don't kill your son!
Jesus came to live with us. He showed us how God loves people
Father, forgive them
He let himself be killed by humans who didn't trust that he was really God. He could have escaped, but he put up with it to conquer the power of evil
VICTORY! Jesus has overcome evil
God loved us so much that he even gave up the son he loved to set us free. Now Jesus is alive in glory He's on our side - evil can't win any more.

Year 2

Genesis 12:1-9; 1 Peter 2:19-end; Matthew 16:13-end

Today is a good opportunity to learn about Abraham. To avoid confusion begin by explaining that Abraham lived many, many years before Jesus was born.

Start with a prayer about trusting and being ready, and a song (e.g. *Forward in faith*).

Then use a model and plasticine or card figures to tell the story of his calling. A green towel or cloth spread over various upturned bowls on a table makes a good landscape.

The children can help prepare it, and put on large stones, pebbles, boxes for buildings and the characters needed:

Abraham
Sarah
his son, Isaac
sheep and cattle
a ram
etc. (farmyard models)

Spend the first half of the session making this model, and when it is all ready, let the children sit round the model while you tell the story of Abraham, moving the figures as you tell it.

At each stage emphasise how Abraham and Sarah trusted God, even when it came to sacrificing their son; and how God rewarded their trust.

Start at Haran, where God makes his promise; *(Genesis 12)*
go on to the oaks of Mamre, where the three visitors tell him his elderly wife will have a son; *(Genesis 18)*
and the birth of Isaac;
then to Moriah (in the mountains)
where God tests Abraham in asking him to sacrifice his son, but provides a ram. *(Genesis 22)*

'ANYONE WHO LOSES HIS LIFE FOR MY SAKE WILL FIND IT.'

Luke 9:23-27

C	D	Y	O	D	E	T	S	E	T
S	A	P	R	F	I	T	C	D	H
S	Y	A	W	K	N	I	F	E	R
R	O	G	S	V	F	B	D	O	J
V	O	N	E	I	A	K	E	D	C
B	Z	A	R	L	I	U	V	O	Q
N	K	C	L	D	T	C	O	G	E
A	A	F	M	J	H	X	L	P	G
S	M	I	M	A	H	A	R	B	A
S	T	O	P	P	E	D	H	N	P

Ha! Ha!
What does that mean?
Whenever we ¢m a h st 4 u
w g against evil, will find b
t it ski hu.
...But we'll be in good company!

GOD TESTED the FAITH of ABRAHAM by asking him to SACRIFICE his only SON, ISAAC. But as Abraham lifted his KNIFE, God STOPPED him from killing his son. He knew now how much Abraham LOVED God.

Genesis 22:1-13

'TAKE UP YOUR CROSS AND FOLLOW ME.'

Matthew 16:24-28

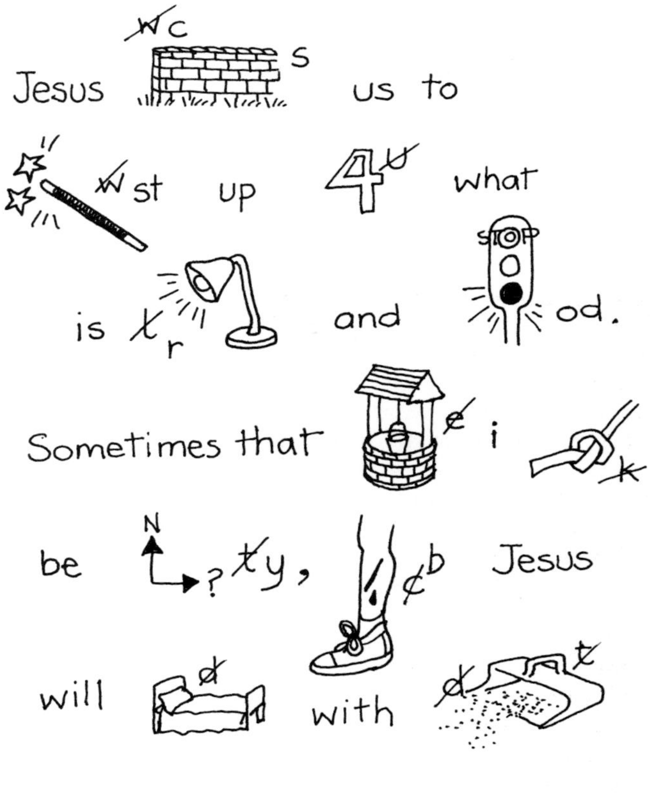
Jesus w c s us to
w st up 4 u what
is t r and STOP od.
Sometimes that e i k
be N ? t y, ¢ b Jesus
will d with d t

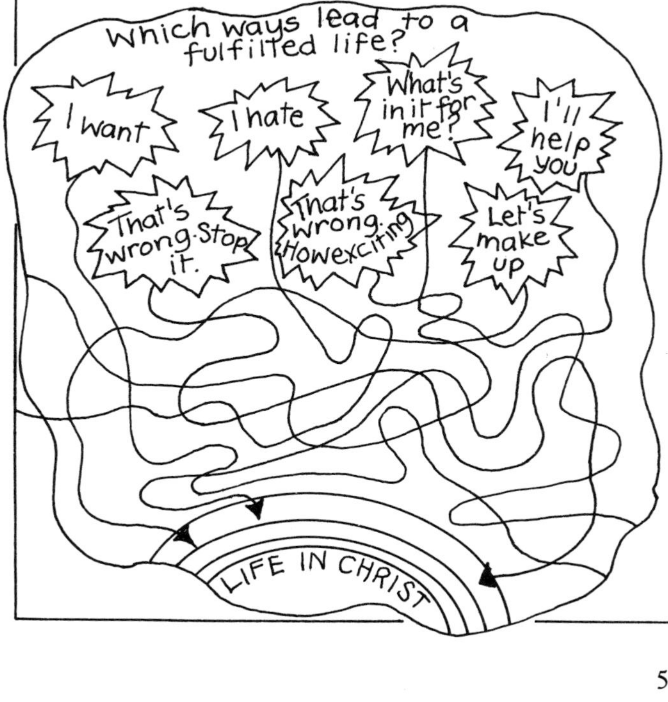
Which ways lead to a fulfilled life?
I want
I hate
What's in it for me?
I'll help you
That's wrong. Stop it.
That's wrong. How exciting
Let's make up
LIFE IN CHRIST

4th SUNDAY IN LENT

Theme: The King and the Kingdom — Transfiguration

Year 1

Exodus 34:29-end; 2 Corinthians 3:4-end; Luke 9:28-36

Tell the story of *the transfiguration.* (Palm Tree's version is *The Secret on the Mountain.*) This works well on tape with music in the background as Jesus is transfigured. Alternatively, have a guitar playing, or taped music while the story is told.

Have the children sitting in a circle round a table with a white candle on it. Have the candle lit as Jesus is transfigured, and blown out when the cloud passes over and only Jesus is left.

Give each child a candle (unlit). Show how one light can light all of these. In the same way, we can all be lit by Jesus.

Give out squares of paper with candle drawn on and slits above.

Ask children to colour the candle and the flame and wick. Stick into books with a strip of sellotape top and bottom. Above it write: 'The bright love of Jesus can light my life.'

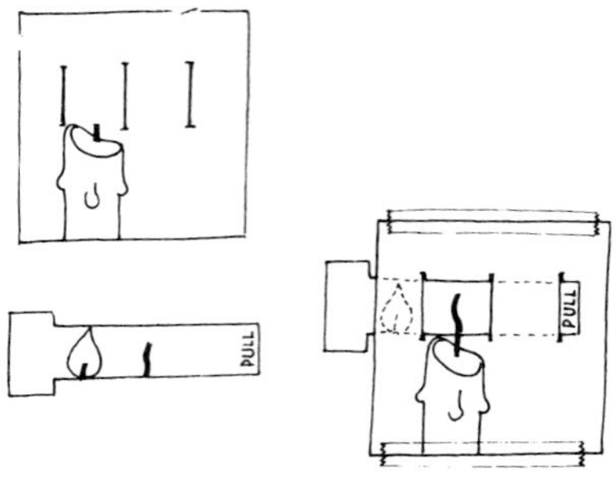
PULL
PULL

Year 2

Exodus 3:1-6; 2 Peter 1:16-19; Matthew 17:1-13

Have lots of candles, flowers and glass in a beautiful arrangement, with quiet music playing as the children come in.

Point out the way the light and beauty is reflected in the glass. Talk about the lovely things in our world which reflect God's glory in this way — sunny days, rain drops, snowflakes, spring flowers, animals, cobwebs etc. — and thank him for them in a prayer or song.

Then tell them how one day, Jesus showed his glory, the glory of God, not as a reflection but directly. Tell the story of the transfiguration as music plays in the background, explaining that God is full of glory like that all the time, even if we only see it sometimes.

Give each child a card folded like this:

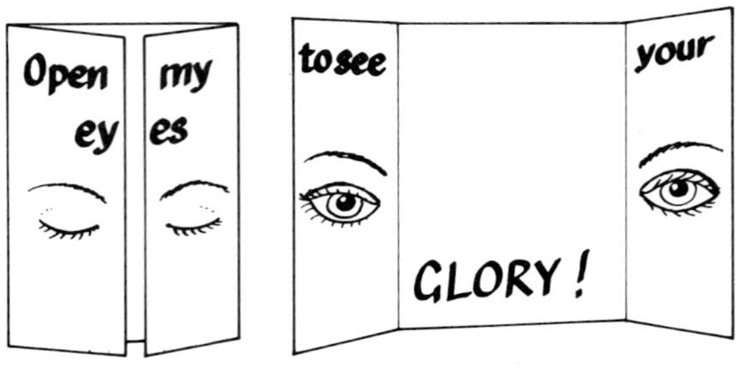
Open
ey
my
es
to see
your
GLORY!

Have the eyes and words already on it. Let them fill the centre with all kinds of lovely things, either drawn, or cut out and stuck on.

'THIS IS MY SON, MY CHOSEN; LISTEN TO HIM.'

Luke 9:28-36

Colour the picture

Peter, James and John were allowed to see the

GLORY

of God's son.

CODE KEY

A	D	E	F	G	H	I	J	L	M	N	O	R	S	T	U
U	T	S	R	O	N	M	L	J	I	H	G	F	E	D	A

They saw Jesus . . .

D	F	U	H	E	R	M	O	A	F	S	T

and talking with . . .

I	G	E	S	E

and

S	J	M	L	U	N

JESUS' FACE SHONE LIKE THE SUN.

Matthew 17:1-13

Join the dots to see what Moses can see

Then colour the picture

Exodus 3:1-6

Jesus was . . .

R
S
I
R

. . . in God's glory

5th SUNDAY IN LENT

Theme: The King and the Kingdom — The Victory of the Cross

Year 1

Exodus 6:2-13; Colossians 2:8-15; John 12:20-32

Show the children a packet of seeds with a picture of the delicious food they will grow into. Sprinkle them into a tray so they can feel them without spilling them. If we put them back into the packet (do so) will they grow? What if we waited for a month or two — would we get a crop then? No, they would just stay as seeds. What needs to happen to them before they will grow?

Bring out a seed tray and a bag of seed compost, a trowel and a watering can, and let the children prepare the seed bed and plant the seeds. Help them to realise that the original seed has to die in order for all the life to come which brings about the harvest. (Keep this tray of seeds watered and cared for week by week, transplanting when necessary, so the children can watch the growing and eventually share the crop.)

Now read or tell the Gospel for today, relating the seeds both to Jesus and to ourselves. Sing *Love is something if you give it away* and give them all some seeds to plant at home. Put the seeds in an envelope on which is written:

PLANTING INSTRUCTIONS
1. Plant your life in Jesus
2. Water it with opportunities to show love kindness and generosity
3. Watch it grow and bear fruit

Year 2

Jeremiah 31:31-34; Hebrews 9:11-14; Mark 10:32-45

Show a few pictures of athletes training, mountaineers climbing, an orchestra practising, or any other activities where hard work or discomfort is necessary for the reward of winning, giving a good performance, or some other worthwhile end.

Discuss times in the children's own lives when they have had to put up with pain or discomfort which was worth doing; getting bruised in the process of learning to ride a bike or skate, for instance. Father Damien, the priest who worked among the lepers in Hawaii, was willing to put up with suffering from leprosy so that the people would be cared for.

When Jesus suffered and died on the cross, it really hurt a lot. But it was worth doing because it led to us being set free from all that is evil and bad.

Help them make this card to take home.

F R E E
JAIL
E V I L
Jesus sets me..

THE LORD HAS RESCUED US FROM DEATH!

1 Colossians 2:13-15

God to the rescue!
Who is he rescuing here?

HE IS RESCUING HIS PEOPLE FROM SLAVERY IN EGYPT
(look in a mirror)

Colour the picture

Exodus 6:2-13

GOD TO THE RESCUE!
WHO IS HE RESCUING HERE?

GOD RESCUES US FROM BEING SLAVES TO SIN ~ HIS DEATH PAID FOR OUR FREEDOM.

DRAW A PICTURE OF YOURSELF HERE

IF YOU WANT TO BE GREAT, BE A SERVANT!

Mark 10:42-45

Sounds odd, doesn't it!
BUT...

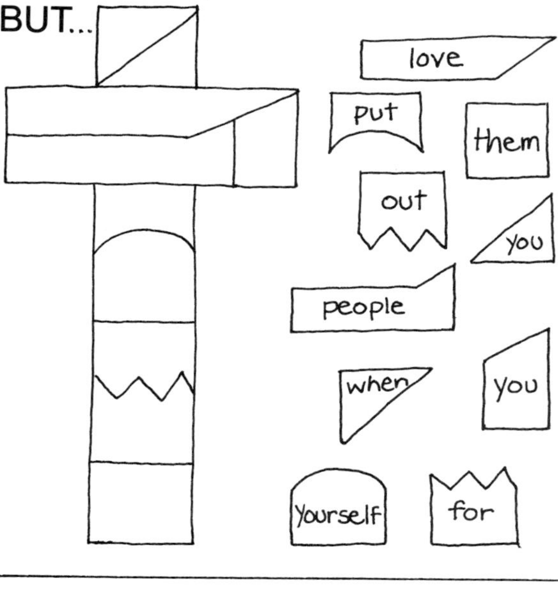

love
put
them
out
you
people
when
you
yourself
for

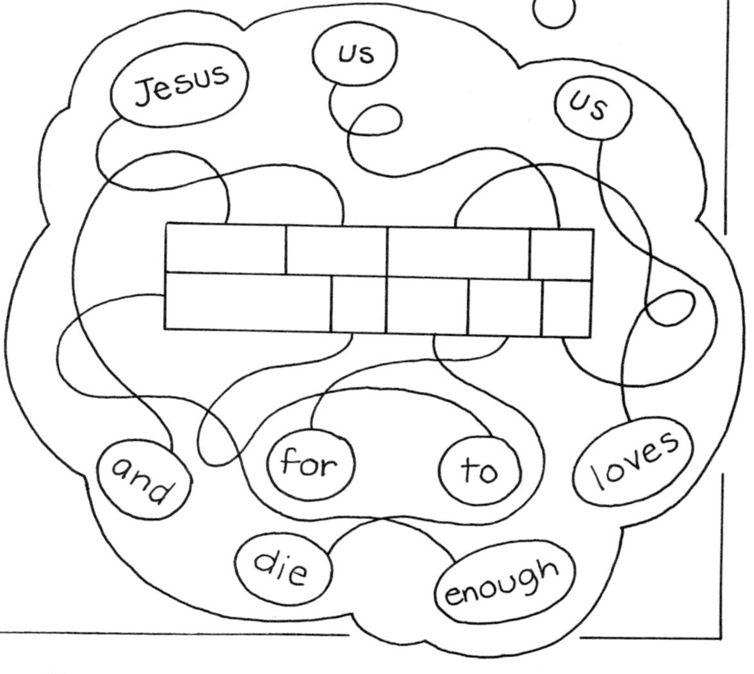

Jesus
us
us
and
for
to
loves
die
enough

PALM SUNDAY

Theme: The Way of the Cross

Years 1 and 2

Isaiah 50:4-9a; Philippians 2:5-11; Mark 14:32-15:41

Encourage the children to bring large leaves or branches to wave in the procession, or colourful streamers. They may also join in the crowd sections of the Gospel if they are in the church at this point.

If not, read *Jesus on a Donkey* (Palm Tree Bible Stories) which tells the story of Jesus entering Jerusalem, and then help the children make a model of that ride. Use a large tray as the base, with hills of crumpled paper under a green towel. The track is a strip of brown or beige material. Houses can be made from white paper like this:

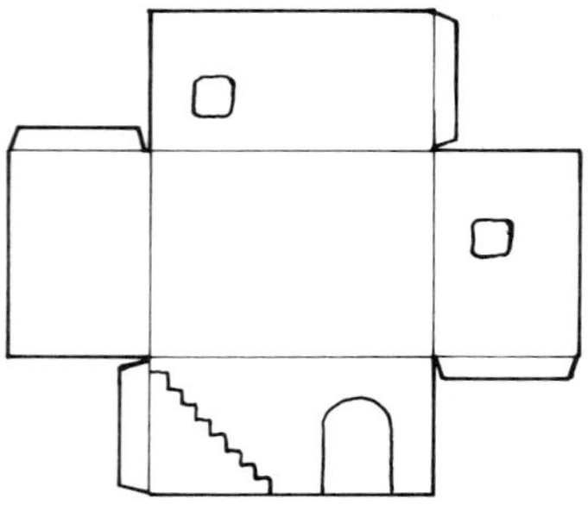

and palm trees from green paper like this:

Have a farmyard model of a donkey and make plasticine figures, waving real leaves. Pieces of material cut out can be laid on the path in front of Jesus.

Display the finished model where the rest of the congregation can see it.

cut out
cut out

Palm Sunday (1) The Way of the Cross

JESUS, THE KING ON A DONKEY!

Matthew 21:1-9

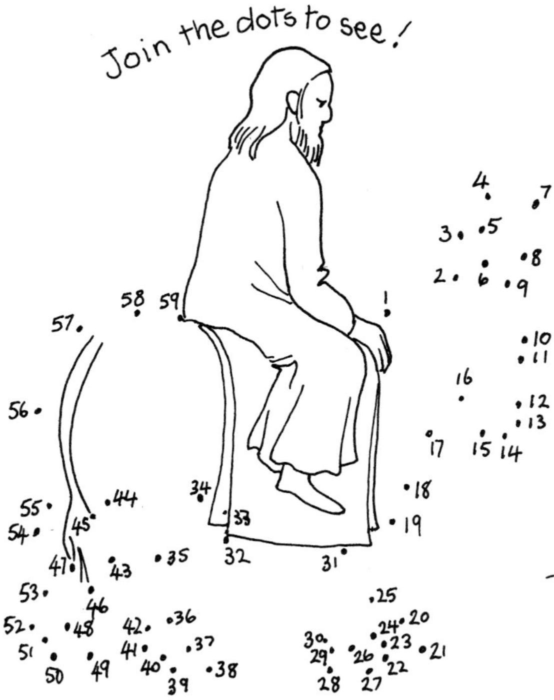
Join the dots to see!

And all the people . . .

AI
EE
+
B
B
EU
+
DY
"
P
D
+NA
2
W
T
N
U
O
D
G
F
GLO
DA
EID
!"

Palm Sunday (2) The Way of the Cross

HOSANNA TO THE KING!

Luke 19:35-38

Colour the picture!

Jesus was riding on a

into

while all the people waved

and cheered him.

Colour the dotted letters.

GOOD FRIDAY

Theme: The Crucifixion

Years 1 and 2

Isaiah 52: 13-53end; Hebrews 10:1-25 or 10:12-22 or 4:14-16; 5:7-9; John 18:1-19:37 or 19:1-37

It is important that children are able to walk their own 'Way of the Cross' today. One way of making this possible is to organise a one or two hour session of teaching, singing and craft activities, with a break for hot cross buns and a drink. A possible programme might be:

10.00 a.m.	Introduction with brief talk *(What happened on Good Friday)*, prayer and a song. Palm Tree's version is called *The Road to the Cross.*
10.25 a.m.	Begin activities
10.45 a.m.	Break; drink and hot cross bun
11.00 a.m.	Resume and complete activities
11.20 a.m.	Gather for short litany, and a song and blessing
11.30 a.m.	End

Possible activities:

a. Make a Holy Week frieze with the crowd, the crosses and the tomb;

b. Make a smaller banner for taking home. Have background material already stitched and figure shapes out of felt. The children assemble it with glue, and thread two sticks through top and bottom, with a piece of wool to hang it up. These could perhaps be blessed at the end.

c. A standing cross could be made from wood. Have ready the base blocks and cross pieces. The children sand the wood down, glue and nail together and varnish. N.B. Very careful supervision necessary!

d. Blow eggs (piece both ends with a needle, and blow contents into a bowl). Then decorate on them a cross made of flowers, coloured with felt tip pens. Use this as a symbol of Christ's death bringing new life. Make a holder for the egg from a small box covered and stuck with coloured paper, and filled with cotton wool.

The atmosphere should be calm and quiet, with the activities being looked on as part of their worship.

Good Friday (1/2) The Crucifixion

HE DIED THAT WE
MIGHT BE FORGIVEN.
Hebrews 10:9-12

EASTER DAY

Theme: The Resurrection

Years 1 and 2

Isaiah 12 or Exodus 14:15-22 or Isaiah 43:16-21; Revelation 1:10-18 or 1 Corinthians 15:12-20 or Colossians 3:1-11; Matthew 28:1-10 or John 20:1-10 (or 1-18) or Mark 16:1-8

Read the first part of *Jesus is Risen* (Palm Tree Bible Stories) or tell the story in your own words, acting it out with plasticine models on a tray with a stone 'cave' built on it in a garden.

Sing one of the Easter songs together and give each child a margarine tub with oasis in it, a selection of Spring flowers and a tall white candle.

Help them make an arrangement of joy at Jesus being alive forever. When they have finished, light all the candles, and let the children carry them in procession into the church near the altar.

Easter Day (1/2) The Resurrection

JESUS IS ALIVE!

Luke 24:33-34

E	I	B	Q	R	O	L	L	E	D
F	A	E	J	E	S	U	S	X	Y
M	O	R	N	I	N	G	W	P	A
C	V	G	L	E	D	O	H	D	D
U	L	T	M	Y	V	C	T	H	N
Z	T	O	K	B	A	I	I	S	U
M	W	M	S	J	O	W	L	R	S
A	N	B	L	E	G	N	A	A	F
E	G	D	E	S	I	M	O	R	P

EARLY on SUNDAY MORNING the WOMEN went to the TOMB. They found the STONE had been ROLLED AWAY. An ANGEL told them that JESUS was ALIVE again, just as he had PROMISED! Mark 16:1-8

1st SUNDAY AFTER EASTER

Year 1 Theme: The Upper Room

Exodus 15:1-11; Peter 1:3-9; John 20:19-29

Begin by passing round a 'feeling' bag with a couple of objects inside it, such as a sieve and a marble, for instance. Each child has a turn to feel the bag and guess what the objects are, but the guesses aren't shared until everyone has had a go.

Then each one says: 'I believe there's a . . . in the bag'. Take the objects out to see who's right, and talk about how they didn't know for sure what was there until they saw it, but they could believe it by using clues, such as what it felt like.

Display a large sign: 'I believe Jesus is God's Son.'

How do we know?

Have we actually seen him?

What clues do we use, then?

Talk about the record of his friends in the Bible, the way Jesus helps us to be kind when we feel like being nasty, (so long as we ask him); the way he helps us through sad or painful times; and the happy feeling we have when we enjoy the lovely world with him.

Then read the Thomas section of *Jesus is Risen* and give the children a picture of this to colour, with Thomas's prayer on it. Encourage them to use this prayer themselves in church or at home.

Year 2 Theme: The Bread of Life

Exodus 16:2-15; 1 Corinthians 15:53-end; John 6:32-40

Remind the children of how the people were fed by Jesus, and say together the prayer written on the loaves and fishes which were made in the Children's Teaching for the 3rd Sunday after the Epiphany. Tell them how the people all got into boats and followed Jesus to Capernaum (a map is useful). What do they think the people were hoping Jesus might do? Feed them with a meal again? They may have an uncle or family friend who often gives them a treat, so they hope for one whenever they meet.

Jesus tells them he has come to give them food that will not leave them hungry a few hours later (we may eat breakfast, but we still need more food by lunchtime), and he calls this the 'bread of life'. Now read the last section of the Gospel, from "Sir," they said.'

Finish with a bread-making session, using a quick-action bread mix. Each child can then take some bread home to share with the family.

Look
Jesus
here
I
am
Use
me

Easter 1 (1) The Upper Room

JESUS CAME AND STOOD AMONG THEM.

John 20:19-29

Q. What did Jesus give them?

A.

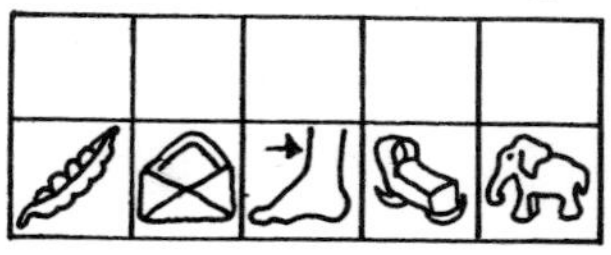

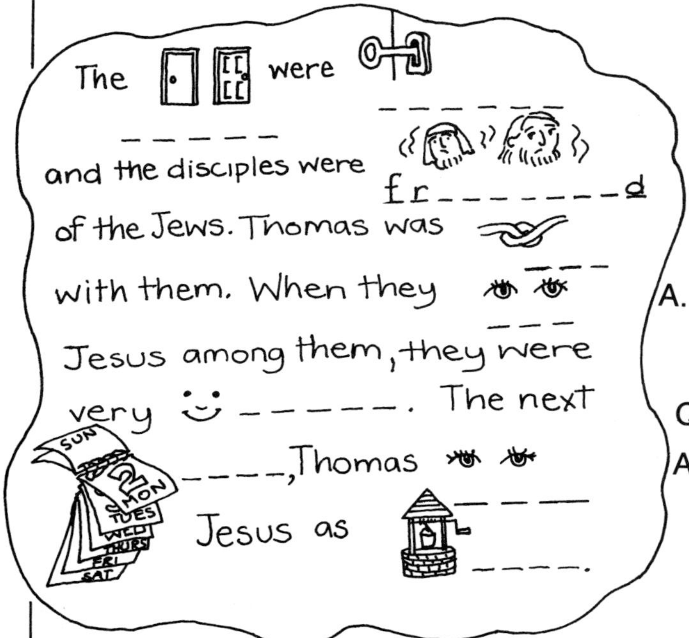

The [ ] were [ ] _ _ _ _ _ _
and the disciples were [ ] fr _ _ _ _ _ _ _d
of the Jews. Thomas was [ ] _ _ _
with them. When they [ ] _ _ _
Jesus among them, they were
very [ ] _ _ _ _ _. The next
_ _ _ _, Thomas [ ] _ _ _ _
Jesus as [ ] _ _ _ _.
SUN
MON
TUES
WED
THURS
FRI
SAT

Q. What did Jesus show Thomas?
(he will give it to us as well, if we ask him)

A.

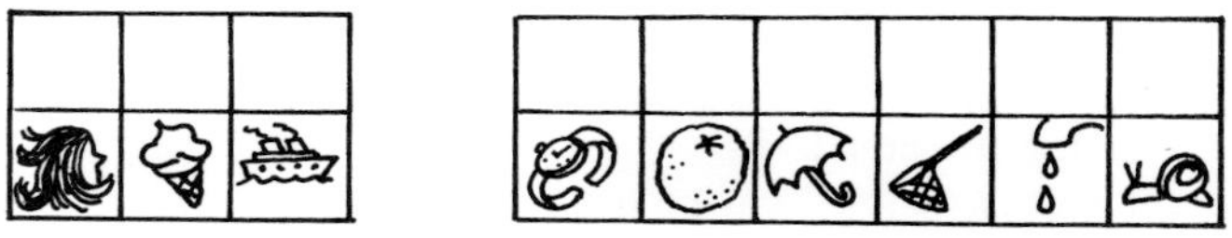

Q. What did Thomas say?

A. 5 9 | 4 7 8 2 | 1 6 2 | 5 9 | 3 7 2

A	D	G	L	M	N	O	R	Y
1	2	3	4	5	6	7	8	9

Easter 1 (2) The Bread of Life

'I AM THE BREAD OF LIFE.'

John 6:34-35

When did you last eat BREAD? ____________

When will you eat it again? ____________

Why do you eat?

____

The people didn't know what it was, so they called it MANNA, which means:

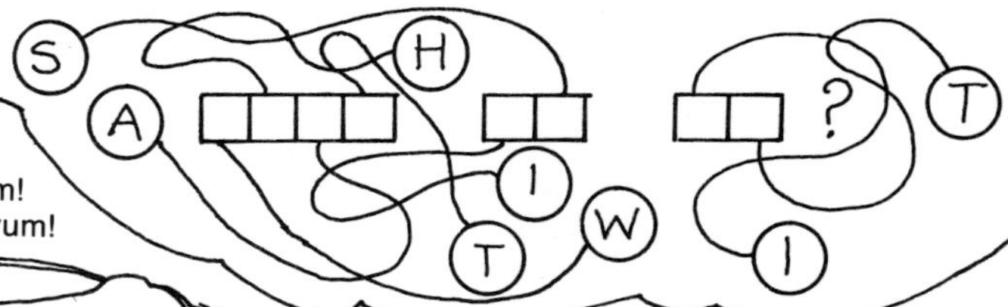

S
H
A
?
T
I
W
T
I

Exodus 16:2-15

yum! yum!
BREAD
we need to feed our

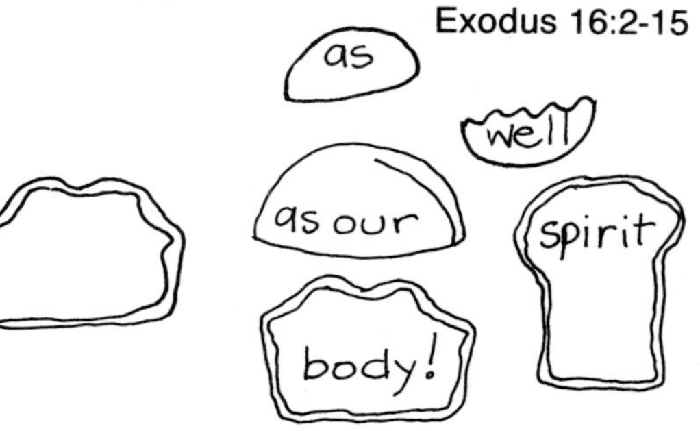

as
well
as our
spirit
body!

2nd SUNDAY AFTER EASTER

Year 1 Theme: The Emmaus Road

Isaiah 25:6-9; Revelation 19:6-9; Luke 24:13-35

Read the Emmaus section of *Jesus is Risen* which captures the atmosphere very well. Talk about the story with the children:

- why do they think the disciples couldn't believe Jesus had risen?
- do they sometimes wonder if it is all true, and then later feel certain of Jesus being with them?
- talk about having expectations (for Christmas presents, for instance) which make us feel let down when they are not what we had in mind.
- when have they been surprised by God acting in their lives?

Teachers can give great encouragement in faith by being prepared to talk about some of their own surprises and disappointments; the children are then brought into contact with the real, living faith, rather than history. Help the children make this pop-up scene of Jesus breaking bread.

They knew him in the
breaking of bread
They knew him in the
breaking of bread
glue on back

Year 2 Theme: The Good Shepherd

Ezekiel 34:7-16; 1 Peter 5:1-11; John 10:7-16

Have a green sheet of paper on the table with some farmyard models of sheep and lambs, a sheepdog and a shepherd. (Britain Toys make a good one.) Talk with the children about what a shepherd's job involves. Some of them may have watched sheep being moved from one pasture to another. What would happen to the sheep if there was no shepherd? Talk about the way they stray into danger, and other ways they are vulnerable.

Now build a model of a sheep fold, or pen, which is used in the country Jesus lived in. Make it from small stones or from plasticine which has been given a stone pattern. The shepherd lay in the doorway to sleep, so he was the door! That kept the sheep all safe inside.

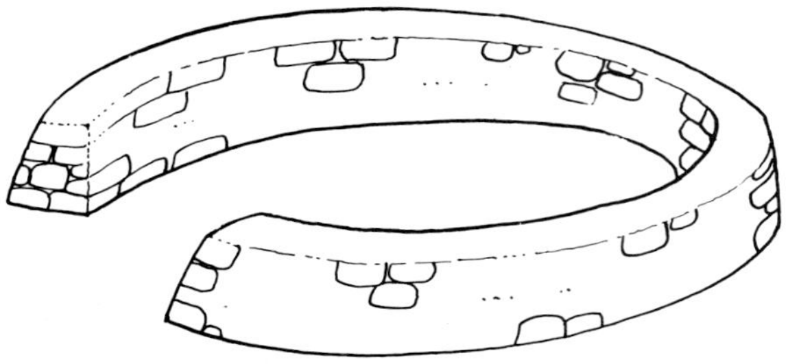

Next read the first part of today's Gospel, and help them understand that Jesus is the Good Shepherd and we are the sheep and lambs.

Then help the children to make sheep headgear on which is written: 'The Lord is my Shepherd'. Perhaps they could process, bleating, into church and kneel for a moment of silence in front of the altar before joining their families.

The Lord is my Shepherd
Tie at back of head

White socks

Easter 2 (1) The Emmaus Road

THEIR EYES WERE OPENED AND THEY RECOGNISED JESUS.

Luke 24:30-31

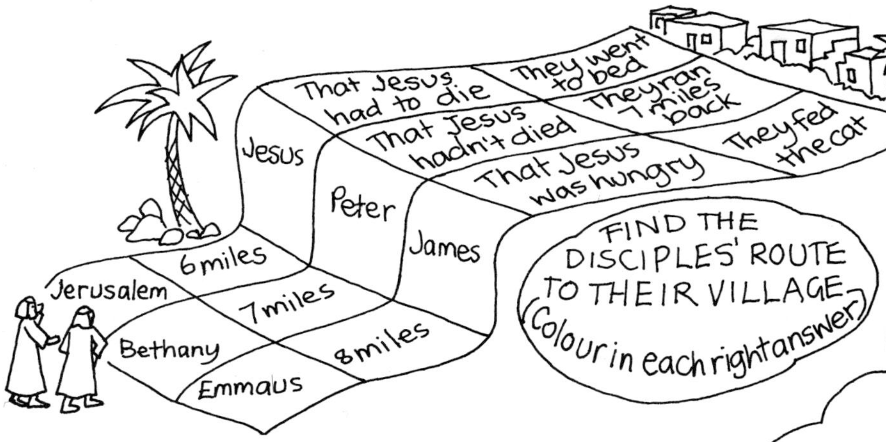

That Jesus had to die
They went to bed
That Jesus hadn't died
They ran 7 miles back
They fed the cat
That Jesus was hungry
Jesus
Peter
James
6 miles
7 miles
8 miles
Jerusalem
Bethany
Emmaus
FIND THE DISCIPLES' ROUTE TO THEIR VILLAGE (Colour in each right answer)

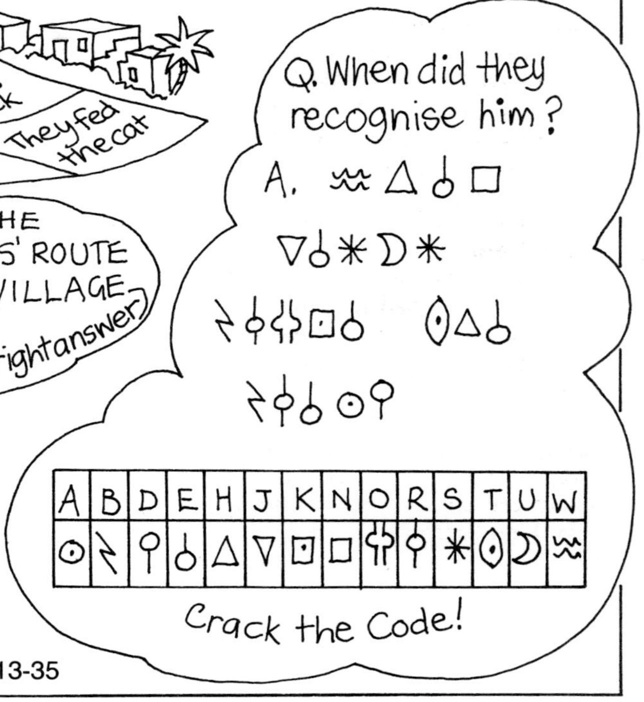

Q. When did they recognise him?
A.
A B D E H J K N O R S T U W
Crack the Code!

1. Where did these two disciples live?
2. How far from home were they?
3. Who joined them as they walked?
4. What did he explain?
5. What did they do when they recognised him?

Luke 24:13-35

Easter 2 (2) The Good Shepherd

JESUS SAID, 'I AM THE GOOD SHEPHERD.'

John 10:7-16

*What makes a good shepherd? (Cross out the things that don't)

SELFISH WATCHFUL STRONG CRUEL GREEDY CARING RELIABLE KIND LAZY BRAVE CARELESS

How many sheep?
There are sixteen sheep.

We are Jesus' sheep and lambs.
Join the dots to make the picture

3rd SUNDAY AFTER EASTER

Year 1 Theme: The Lakeside

Isaiah 61:1-7; 1 Corinthians 15:1-11; John 21:1-14

Use the Gospel and tell the story of the disciples fishing and seeing Jesus on the beach.

Divide the group into two. One group prepares the acting out (give lots of help and encourage the shy ones to participate).

The other group cuts out lots of fish, all different colours, shapes and sizes. Have a net (old curtain) and an upturned table as a boat. Then the actors perform to the fish makers.

If this were prepared beforehand, the children could present their performance during the Gospel. Otherwise, let them take a fish home with them to remind them of what happened. Suggest they tell their families, or draw a picture of it to bring back next week.

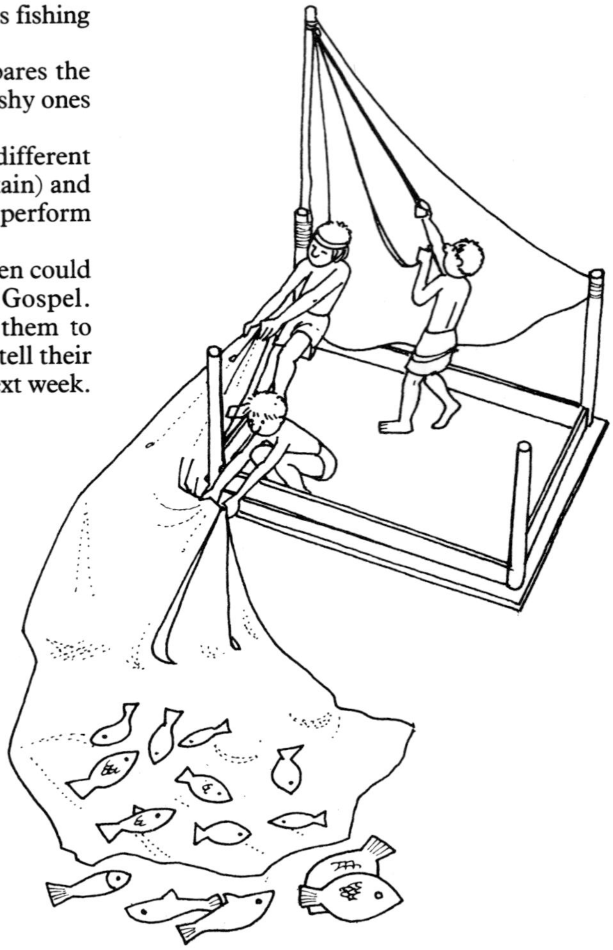

Year 2 Theme: The Resurrection and the Life

1 Kings 17:17-end; Colossians 3:1-11; John 11:17-27

Tell the children the story in today's Gospel using an overhead projector or cereal packet 'television'. Explain that God not only brings life, he actually is life. You could sing *Lord of the Dance* which expresses this idea.

Greaseproof paper

Then let the children cut out, colour and staple together these two pictures to show the effect of God's love.

JESUS IS ALIVE — AND COOKING BREAKFAST!

In the SEA of TIBERIAS, PETER and his FRIENDS went fishing, but they CAUGHT NOTHING. Then they saw JESUS standing on the BEACH. He had lit a FIRE. He told them to FISH on the right SIDE of the BOAT. They caught lots of fish and ATE some for breakfast with Jesus.

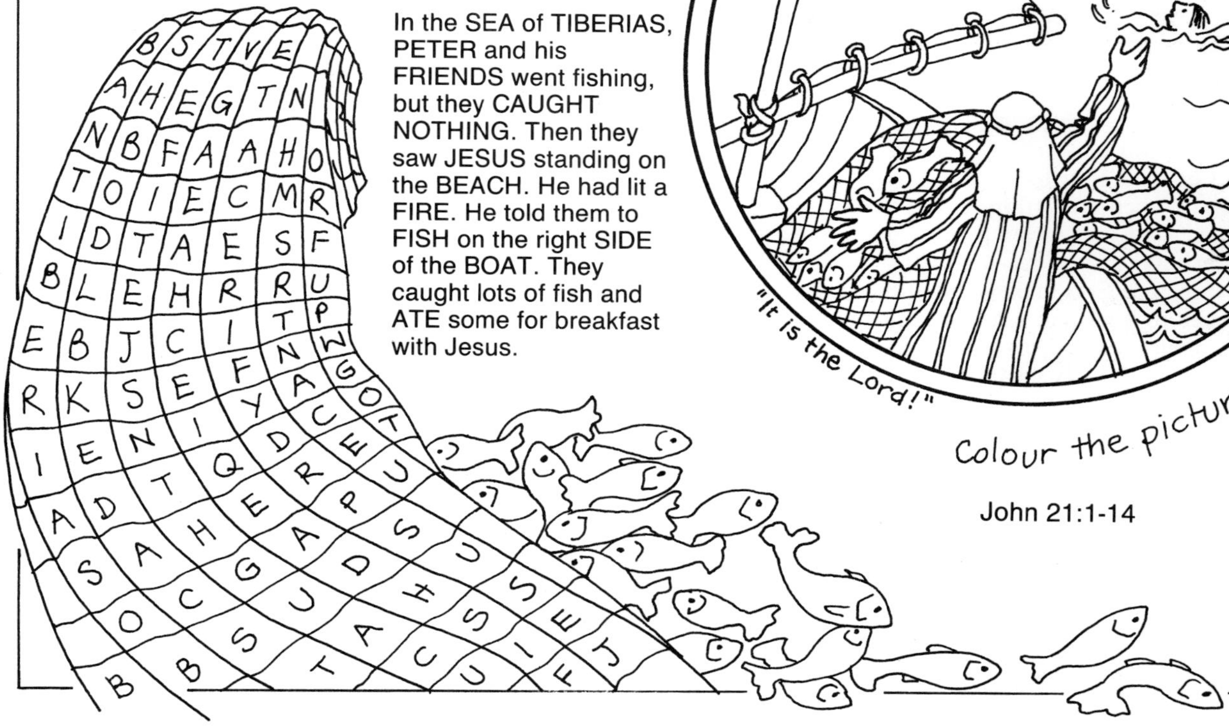

"It is the Lord!"

Colour the picture

John 21:1-14

JESUS SAID, 'I AM THE RESURRECTION AND THE LIFE!

John 11:17-27

LAZARUS IS BROUGHT TO LIFE

A	R	C	S	O	N	M	H	D	D
S	E	K	I	B	W	O	D	I	W
D	H	B	R	E	A	T	H	E	U
A	T	P	E	C	A	D	G	D	J
I	O	N	R	L	H	O	U	S	E
L	M	B	I	A	I	W	D	T	T
L	Q	V	J	B	Y	H	Q	H	K
Z	E	I	X	O	V	E	R	E	N
D	L	I	H	C	F	E	D	A	S
E	O	Y	G	R	E	U	M	W	P

The SON of a WIDOW got ILL and DIED. ELIJAH was staying at the HOUSE at the time. Elijah PRAYED and stretched himself over the child THREE times. The CHILD started to BREATHE again. Elijah brought him to his MOTHER. "Look," he said, "your son is ALIVE!"

1 Kings 17:17-end

4th SUNDAY AFTER EASTER

Year 1 Theme: The Charge to Peter

Isaiah 62:1-5; Revelation 3:14-end; John 21:15-22

Remind the children of how Peter had denied Jesus three times when he was frightened of what might happen to him if he told the truth. Discuss times when we feel scared of doing the right thing (like owning up, for instance) and how we don't feel really comfortable with someone we have hurt until we've said sorry and they have forgiven us.

Now tell or read how Jesus puts things right again for Peter, and even trusts him again. Jesus does the same with us — he will always give us another chance.

Help each child make a zig-zag picture to show how turning away from God makes him and us miserable. Turning back to him makes him and us happy. Each picture is coloured, cut in strips and pasted on to thin card in the order: 1A 2B 3C 4D etc. Fold the finished card like a fan, and the two pictures will emerge when viewed from one side or the other.

1 2 3 4 5 6 7 8 9 10 11 12
A B C D E F G H I J K L

Year 2 Theme: The Way, the Truth, and the Life

Proverbs 4:10-19; 2 Corinthians 4:13-5:5; John 14:1-11

Working on the theme of Jesus being 'The Way', begin by setting up two model villages, built by the children in lego or building blocks, in different parts of the room.

When they are finished, sit down with the children between the villages and talk about how the people could get from one to the other, through the wild countryside. They could have little arrows at intervals — but in fog you might get lost between the signs. They could have instructions, like: 'turn left at the second tree' — but suppose the wind blew a tree down, or another one grew up? You could lose your way.

What we really need is a clear road or track to walk along, which goes directly to the distant town. (Draw a road in chalk.) Now tell the children how Jesus said he was the Way, or road, to God in heaven, so if we want to get there we just have to follow him.

Help them make a spiritual map, with Baptism town at one corner, and The Heavenly City at another. The way winds round all kinds of dangerous mountains, rushing rivers, thick forests etc., but never disappears until it reaches the City. Along the road they write in: Jesus said, 'I am the Way'. Colour in the maps and display them in church if possible.

Try singing: *One more step along the road I go* or *Forward in faith* (MWTP, 54).

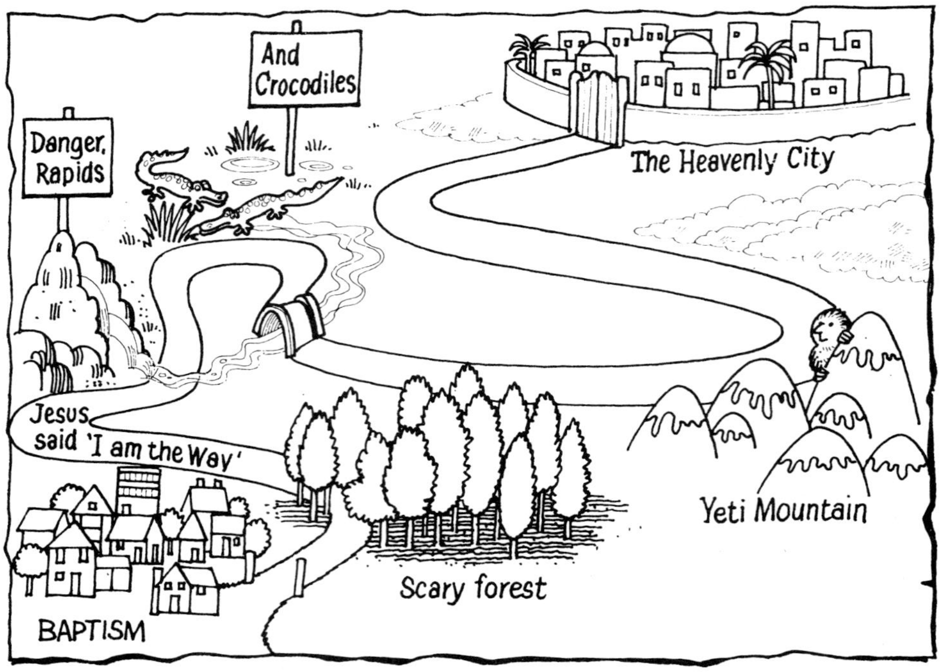
And Crocodiles
Danger, Rapids
The Heavenly City
Jesus said 'I am the Way'
Yeti Mountain
Scary forest
BAPTISM

Easter 4 (1) The Charge to Peter

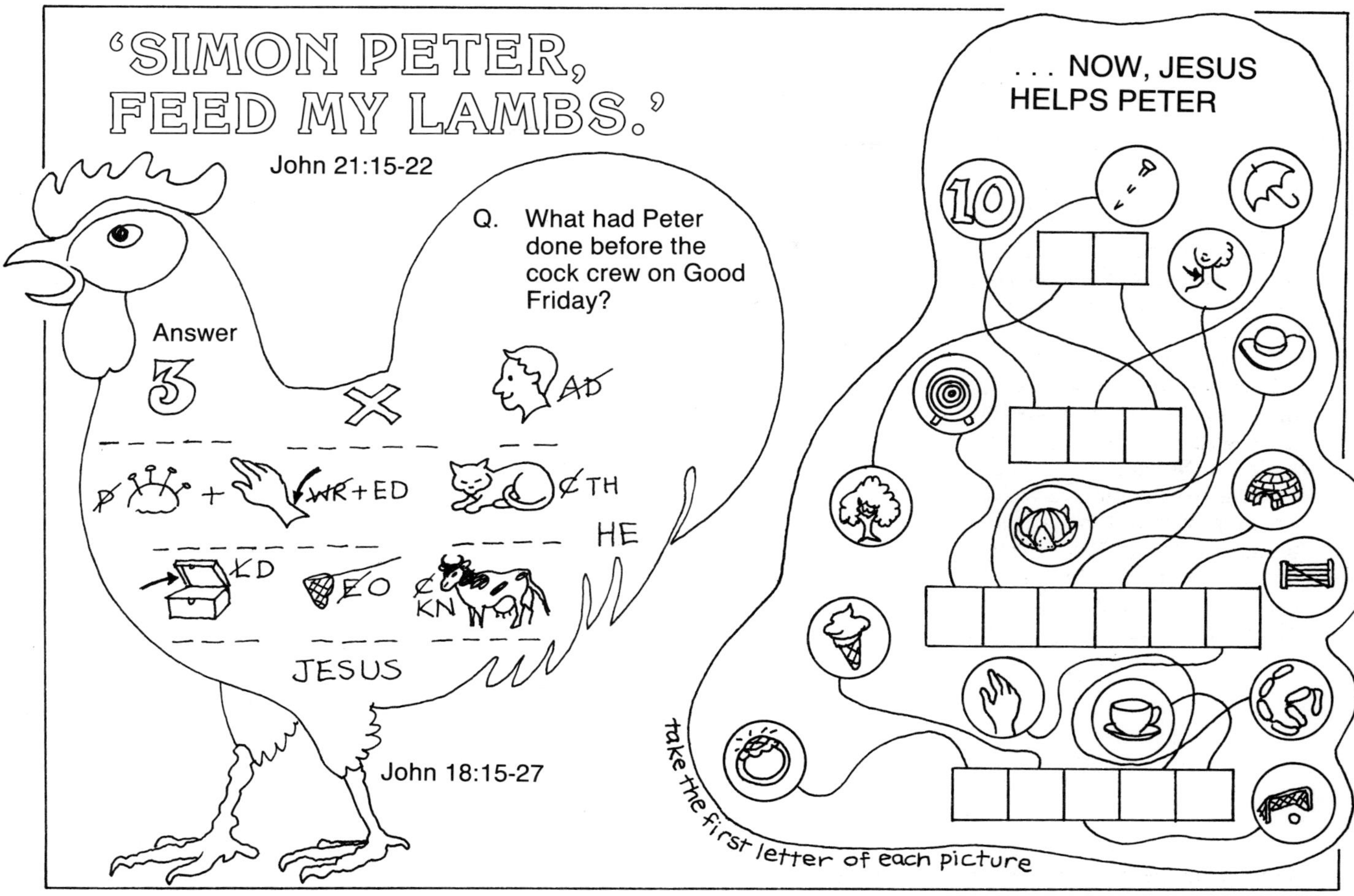

'SIMON PETER, FEED MY LAMBS.'
John 21:15-22
Q. What had Peter done before the cock crew on Good Friday?
Answer
3
AD
ED
TH
HE
KD
EO
KN
JESUS
John 18:15-27
. . . NOW, JESUS HELPS PETER
10
take the first letter of each picture

Easter 4 (2) The Way, the Truth, and the Life

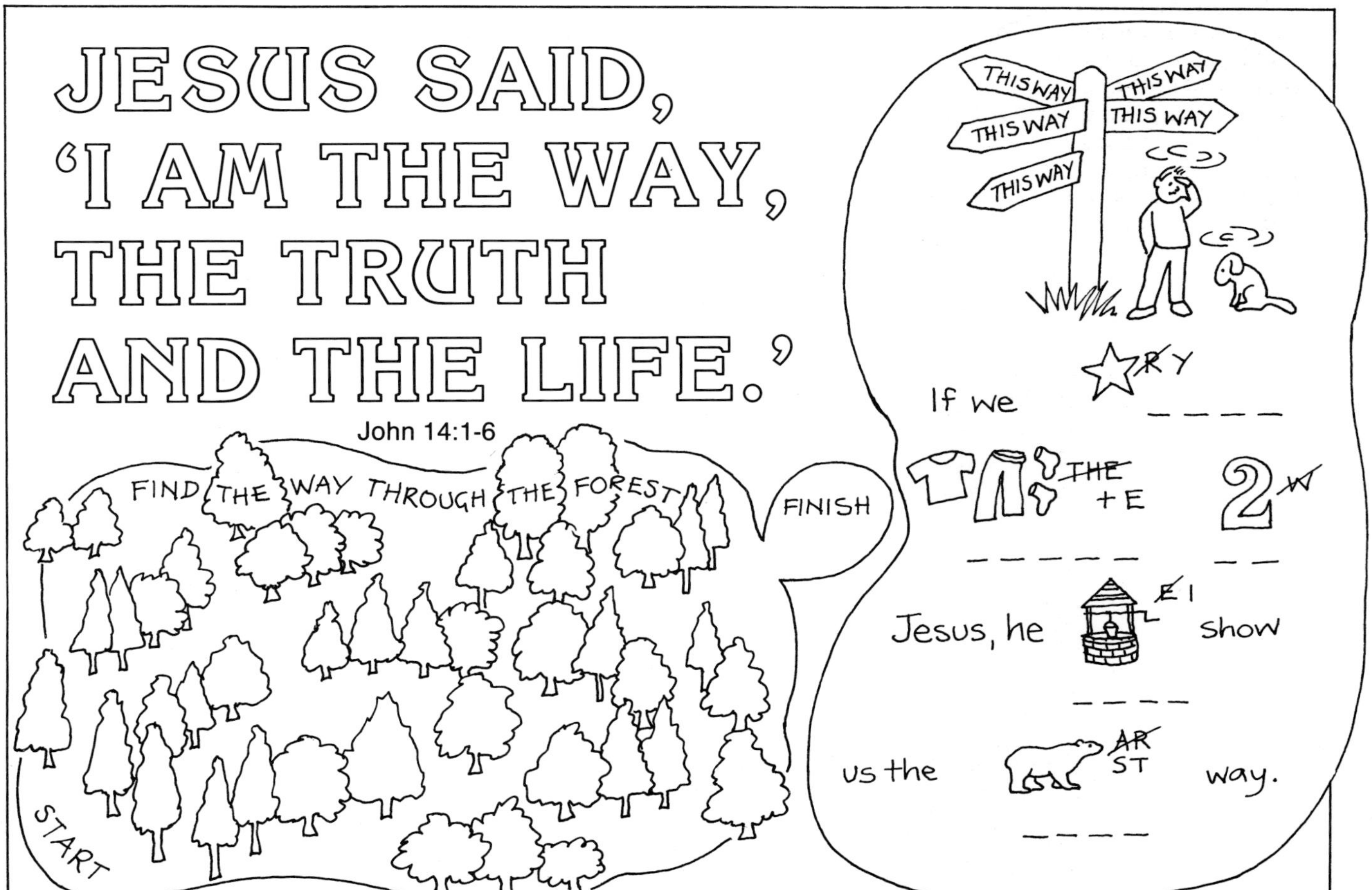

JESUS SAID, 'I AM THE WAY, THE TRUTH AND THE LIFE.'
John 14:1-6
FIND THE WAY THROUGH THE FOREST
START
FINISH
THIS WAY
THIS WAY
THIS WAY
THIS WAY
THIS WAY
If we
RY
THE
+E
2
W
Jesus, he
EI
show
us the
AR
ST
way.

5th SUNDAY AFTER EASTER

Theme: Going to the Father

Year 1

Hosea 6:1-6; 1 Corinthians 15:21-28; John 16:25-end

Have ready an assortment of pictures and newspaper cuttings about good and bad things in our world. Talk with the children about some of the very good things in the world. Is it all good? What sort of bad things happen? (Wars, not enough food for some, quarrels, selfishness, crimes etc.) Read them the words of Jesus: 'In the world you will have trouble. But courage! The victory is mine; I have conquered the world.' So although there are bad things, and some of them will happen to us during life, God's goodness has already won over evil, so evil can NEVER win. Sing *I have a friend who is deeper than the ocean* (MWTP,96) and give each child a duplicated paper, personalised with his or her own name.

Don't be afraid, ...,
because I will look after you
and keep you safe.
You stick up for me
and I will stick up for you.
Together we'll make the world
a happier place.

They can decorate it and keep it to read whenever they need courage to do the right thing.

Year 2

Deuteronomy 34; Romans 8:28-end; John 16:12-24

Talk with the children about how we can keep in touch with people when they are in different places; for example: radio, telephone, radar, letters. Talk about when these aids are used for space travel, docking a ship, in aeroplanes, or at other times when it would be dangerous to act without the guidance of someone who can see better than we can, and who knows all the relevant information.

In life, God is at the base control, and can see the whole picture of what is happening — not just our little bit of it. He is able and willing to guide us through and stay in close contact all the time. Now show them a telephone. What do we have to do to get in touch with someone at the other end of the line? Explain that although God is always in touch with us, we won't be able to talk to him and listen to him unless we keep in touch from our end, too. And that's what praying is.

Help the children make yoghurt pot telephones. Write on them at one end: 'Don't forget to keep in touch with God' and at the other end: 'God always listens'.

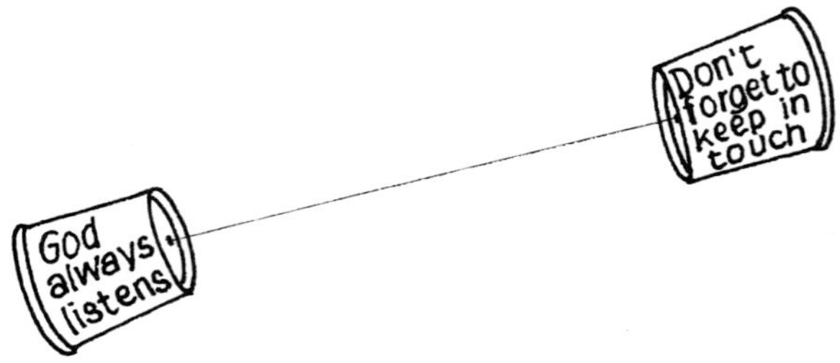
Don't forget to keep in touch
God always listens

Easter 5 (1) Going to the Father

HAVE COURAGE — I HAVE CONQUERED THE WORLD!

John 16:33

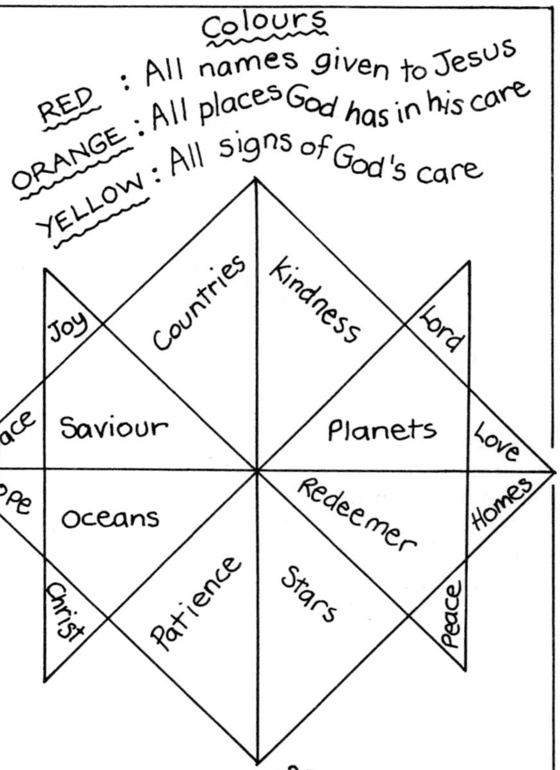
Colours
RED : All names given to Jesus
ORANGE : All places God has in his care
YELLOW : All signs of God's care
Joy
Countries
Kindness
Lord
Space
Saviour
Planets
Love
Hope
Oceans
Redeemer
Homes
Christ
Patience
Stars
Peace

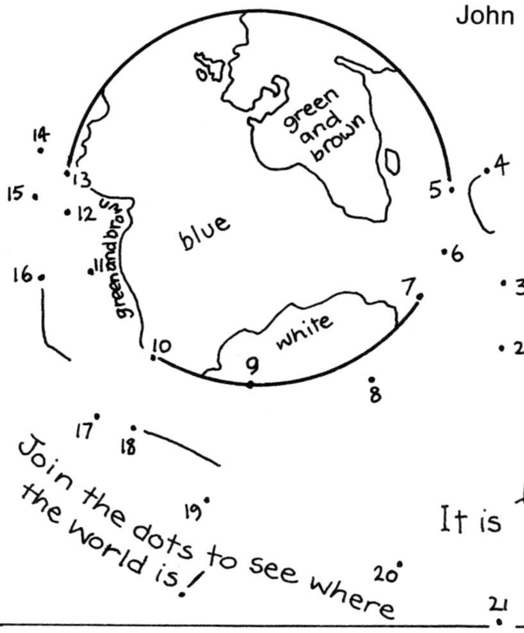
green and brown
blue
green and brown
white
Join the dots to see where the world is!

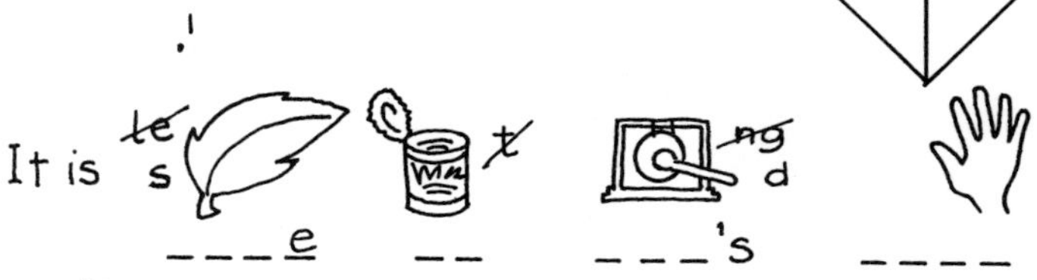
It is
te
s
t
ng
d
___e
__
___'s
____

Easter 5 (2) Going to the Father

NOTHING CAN SEPARATE US FROM GOD'S LOVE!

Romans 8:38-39

Q. Where did Jesus say he was going?
A. He said he was going
b
p
tt
s
b
f+er
b
sh
__
___
______
__
__a___.

John 16:28

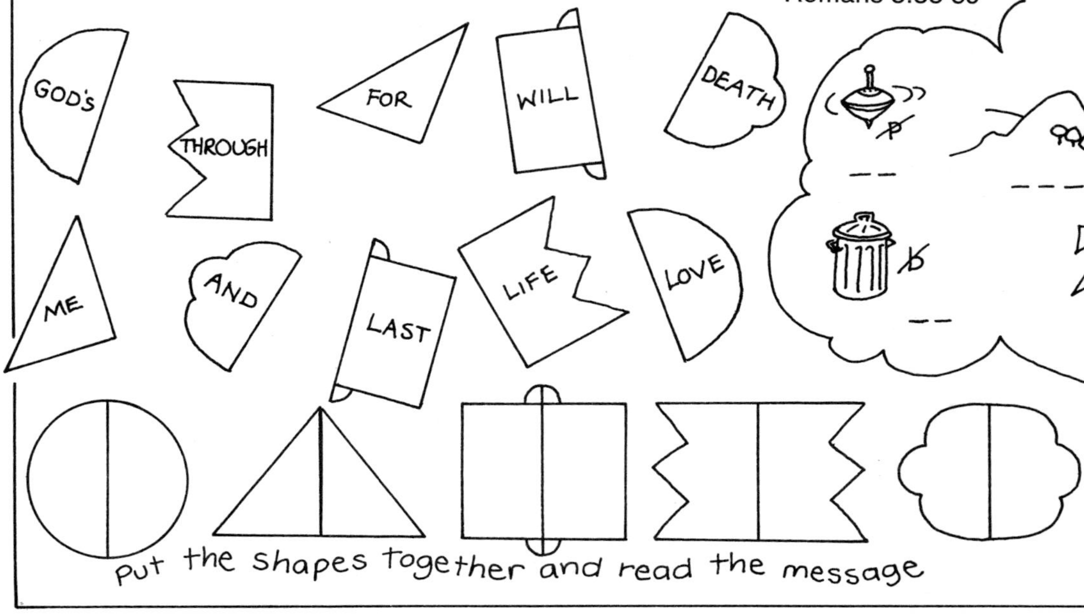
GOD'S
THROUGH
FOR
WILL
DEATH
ME
AND
LAST
LIFE
LOVE
Put the shapes together and read the message

SUNDAY AFTER ASCENSION DAY

Theme: The Ascension of Christ

Year 1

Daniel 7:9-14; Ephesians 1:15-end; Luke 24:45-end

It is not widely known that children are still entitled to take time off from school on Ascension Day in order to go to church. If you decide to have a special children's service, make out a form for the children to take into school and use the occasion to witness through courtesy and goodwill.

Keep the service simple and involve the children in the planning, reading, singing and decorating.

For the Sunday after Ascension, start by showing the children a bright cut-out sun, then cover it from sight with a cut-out cloud. Is the sun still there? Show that it is. We do not always see it because it is sometimes hidden from view, but we know it is always there. How?

Talk about life and growth and light and warmth. If we shut ourselves in where the sun cannot reach us we couldn't survive. Can we see Jesus? No. Then what do we mean when we say he is alive? Where is he?

Read them an account of the Ascension as told in Acts. His friends had seen him a lot after he had come back to life on the first Easter Day, and now, like the sun behind a cloud, he is hidden from sight for a time. (Show a bright card with JESUS written on it, and put the cloud in front.) But he is just as much alive as before. As our King he reigns over everything — people, animals, the sun, the stars, the universe!

Ask some children to draw and colour flowers and trees, some animals and people, some stars and planets, mountains, seas and weather. Then mount all their work on a big collage banner, with OUR GOD REIGNS written over the top. This can be carried into the church in procession.

OUR GOD
REIGNS

Year 2

2 Kings 2:1-15; Ephesians 4:1-13; Luke 24:45-end

In an effort to steer clear of false impressions, we sometimes avoid teaching children about heaven. Today is a good opportunity to put that right. Start with a game. In a box have slips of paper which describe things in terms of other things:

- a bit like an orange but not so sweet, and coloured yellow;
- a kind of chair which has no back;
- a tall sort of cup;
- a wax stick that you can burn slowly; etc.

Point out that if you had not known before what a lemon was, you would have a better idea now, but not an exact idea until you actually saw a lemon yourself. Show them one. And similarly with the other items described.

It is the same with heaven. Pictures and words in the Bible give us clues but no more.

Show a large round poster with these words written all round the edge:

Then make a collection of words inside the circle which give us an idea of what heaven is like:

- happy
- beauty
- peace
- joy
- no worry
- Daddy finds you when you were lost
- like when you give Nana your best drawing and she's very pleased
- like when your friends ask you to join in their game, etc.

Stress that these are only clues, but try to show them some idea of what being with Jesus means in feelings they can understand, rather than looking at the idea of 'place'.

Let the children decorate the words with lovely bright colours and patterns and if possible display the poster in church.

Heaven is where Jesus is! Where

JESUS WILL COME AGAIN IN GLORY.

Acts 1:11

H	A	E	G	J	O	R	D	P	J
Z	I	R	N	I	S	T	I	E	F
B	D	S	E	N	P	W	S	A	W
S	E	C	V	T	S	U	C	H	T
D	S	Y	A	O	S	L	I	A	B
Q	S	K	E	Q	A	N	P	U	Q
H	E	P	H	G	E	M	L	I	H
N	L	X	I	K	D	E	E	C	W
A	B	B	A	N	R	M	S	P	N
S	J	T	O	D	V	L	Y	O	C

AS JESUS BLESSED HIS DISCIPLES HE WAS TAKEN UP INTO HEAVEN

AS HE BLESSED THEM HE WAS TAKEN UP INTO HEAVEN

Luke 24:50-53

W – WHITE
Y – YELLOW
O – ORANGE
R – RED

COLOUR THE WORDS IN ANY BRIGHT COLOURS

C	O	M	E	A	F	I	Q	W	R
Y	L	X	G	X	S	A	K	I	T
A	O	E	P	W	H	D	S	L	G
O	T	U	B	T	N	J	V	L	U
Y	B	M	D	S	C	G	O	H	N
H	I	M	U	U	O	R	F	E	K
N	Z	S	L	J	Y	E	V	G	V
Q	E	C	M	O	L	A	S	A	W
J	I	I	T	S	E	J	R	U	W
O	T	P	N	H	N	I	A	G	A

'JESUS WILL COME AGAIN IN GLORY JUST AS YOU SAW HIM GO TO HEAVEN.'

PENTECOST

Theme: The Holy Spirit

Years 1 and 2

Genesis 11:1-9 or Exodus 19:16-25; Acts 2:1-11; Acts 2:1-21; John 14:15-26 or 20:19-23

Tell the children what happened at Pentecost, emphasising that Jesus' friends were keeping in touch with him through prayer, so they were prepared when his life, or Spirit, came to them so powerfully. Explain that we need to keep in touch with him, too, if we want him to live in us. (Palm Tree's version of the story is called *Wind and Fire*.)

Talk about qualities the Holy Spirit gives us — love, joy, peace etc. Then help the children to make long streamers out of orange, red and yellow, with these qualities drawn or printed on them. As the children come into church they dance round the aisles waving the streamers and twirling them so they look like fire.

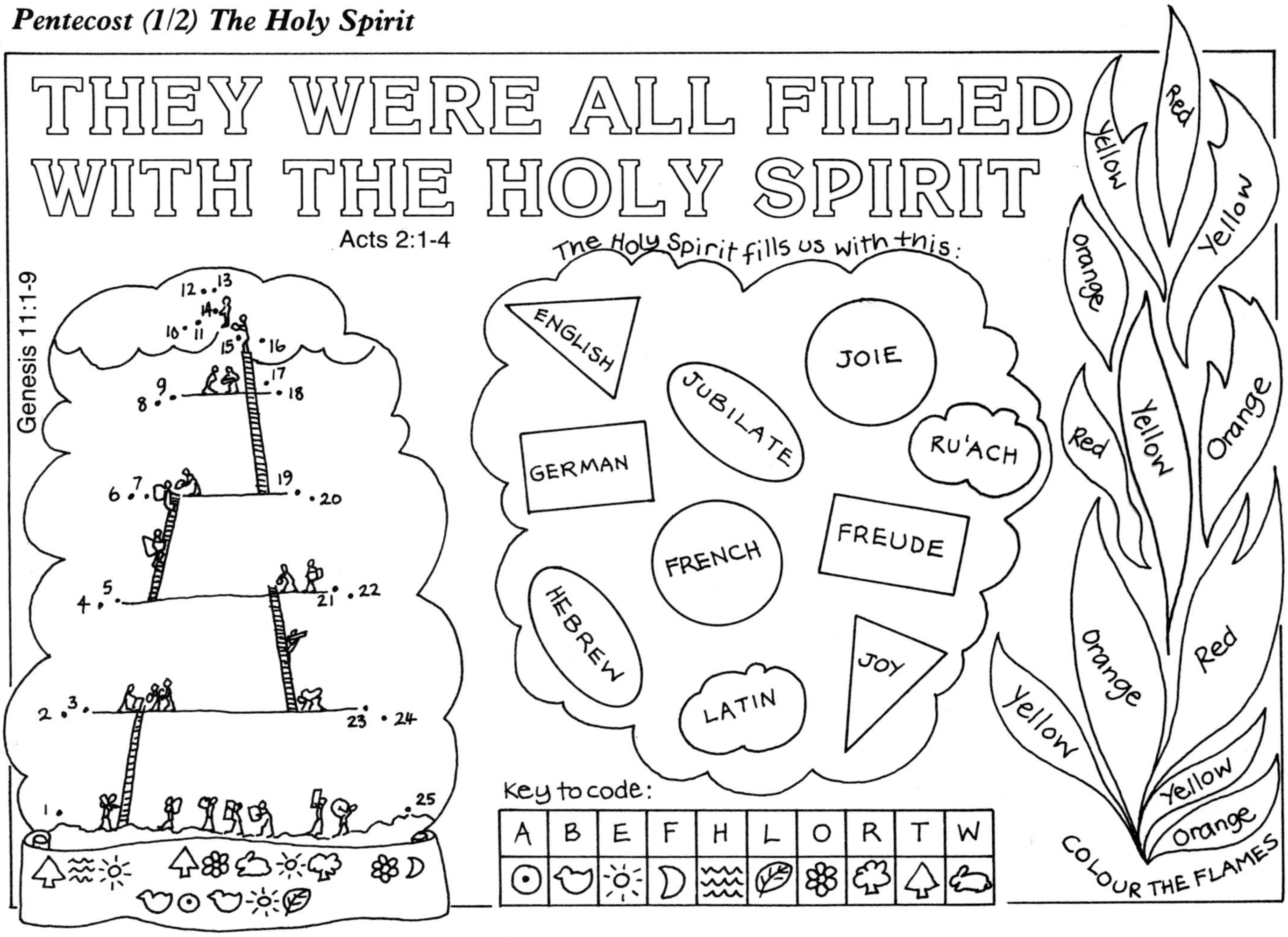
THEY WERE ALL FILLED WITH THE HOLY SPIRIT
Acts 2:1-4
Genesis 11:1-9
The Holy Spirit fills us with this:
ENGLISH
JUBILATE
JOIE
RU'ACH
GERMAN
FRENCH
FREUDE
HEBREW
LATIN
JOY
Key to code:
A B E F H L O R T W
Red
Yellow
Yellow
orange
Red
Yellow
Orange
Orange
Red
Yellow
Yellow
Orange
COLOUR THE FLAMES

TRINITY SUNDAY

Theme: The Trinity

Years 1 and 2

Isaiah 6:1-8; Ephesians 1:3-14; John 14:8-17

Begin by exploring relationships in the group, asking the children to stand in the 'daughter' ring, if they are daughters and the 'son' ring if they are sons (use lengths of wool, or hula hoops to make the rings). Now ask the sisters and brothers to go to other rings, such as cousin, grandchild, friend and nephew. Some children will have changed rings several times.

Sit the children in a circle and show them a picture of someone they all know about — it may be the Queen; or a photo of one of the teachers, perhaps. Work out together all the different things the person is, such as mother, daughter, woman, sister, grandmother, queen, horse rider. Write all these down beside the picture.

Now show them a poster with the word GOD in the middle. Uncover the first picture of trees, mountains, animals and flowers.

What is God?

He is our Father, the Creator.

Uncover the second picture of Jesus, healing and teaching.

What else is God? He is Jesus Christ.

Uncover the third picture of wind and fire and the disciples full of joy, which they will remember from last week.

What else is God? He is the Holy Spirit.

Just as they are themselves, although they are also sisters, friends, and cousins, so God is God, although he is also Father, Son and Holy Spirit. Give each child a triangle of coloured card. They write GOD in the middle and Father, Jesus and Spirit at the three corners to take home with them.

Paper blu-tacked over pictures
GOD

Trinity Sunday (1/2) The Trinity

HOLY!
HOLY!
HOLY!
TRINITY MEANS
TH
B
The Creator FATHER
The saving SON
The lifegiving SPIRIT
GOD IS

2nd SUNDAY AFTER PENTECOST (TRINITY 1)

Year 1 Theme: The People of God

Exodus 19:1-6; 1 Peter 2:1-10; John 15:1-5

Bring along a gardening book with clear illustrations to explain pruning, a pair of secateurs and gardening gloves, and a bunch of grapes.

First put on the gloves and hold the secateurs, and discuss what kind of job you are ready for. If your church has a garden take the children out into it and show them how the roses have been pruned so they produce better flowers. Also find any flower and trace it back to the main stem and roots, from which it gets all its life. Cut off one twig. Will this be able to produce flowers?

Back inside, show the children how gardeners have to learn to prune all their fruit trees and bushes, so as to produce more fruit. Then read today's Gospel, and help the children understand that we need to be (1) joined on to Jesus and (2) pruned, if we are to produce fruit.

On a large sheet of paper draw a central vine with many branches and some leaves. Let the children stick on lots of clusters of grapes which they have coloured and labelled like this:

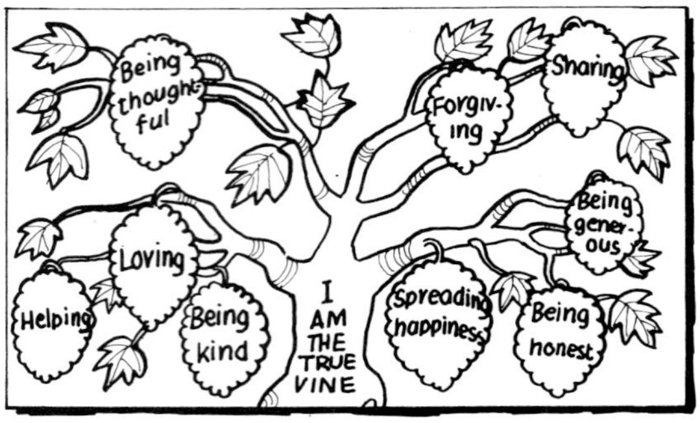
Being thought-ful
Forgiv-ing
Sharing
Being gener-ous
Loving
Helping
Being kind
I AM THE TRUE VINE
Spreading happiness
Being honest

Year 2 Theme: The Church's Unity and Fellowship

2 Samuel 7:4-16; Acts 2:37-end; Luke 14:15-24

Today's Gospel is good to use for making a 'television' programme. The television is a cereal packet with two wooden spoons for winding the 'film' on, and the story is displayed in a series of pictures on a long strip of paper, marked into numbered frames. Either the words can be written underneath each picture, or they can be read on to tape with a clicker between each frame so that the winder knows when to do his bit.

Tell the children the story first and have each part written on a separate card. These are then given out in order to the children, who work on a particular frame, either drawing or colouring in the appropriate picture. It may be easiest to work on the floor, or to stick separate sheets on to a strip when they are finished.

The finished story can be presented to others, perhaps during visits to the elderly, or those in hospital. It can be kept as useful resource material.

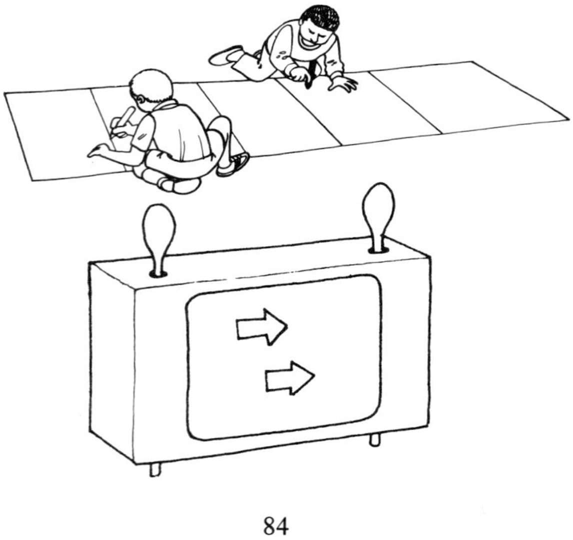

Pentecost 2 (1) The People of God

'I AM THE VINE, YOU ARE THE BRANCHES.'

John 15:5

Fill in the names of some other living stones in the church (don't forget your own name!)
Francis
Peter
Mary
JESUS CHRIST
1 Peter 2:5
Join the grapes to the vine with strong branches
Fit the words in the matching stones to build the message
BUILT
LET
LIVING
INTO
BE
COME
TEMPLE
STONES
YOURSELVES
A
SPIRITUAL
AS
AND

Pentecost 2 (2) The Church's Unity and Fellowship

THEY SHARED THEIR MEALS IN LOVE AND JOY

Acts 2:42-47

Snapshots of the early church
Draw in the pictures
They met often to hear the apostles teach
The apostles brought about many miracles of healing
They broke bread together
They sold all they had and shared all their money
They went to the temple every day

D	N	B	D	E	L	P	P	I	R	C
C	O	B	A	N	Q	U	E	T	A	D
S	N	O	I	T	A	T	I	V	N	I
E	E	A	N	G	R	Y	J	I	K	M
R	E	H	X	F	O	E	L	N	Y	S
V	O	H	Q	G	W	B	T	I	E	L
A	D	O	C	L	E	E	T	S	A	T
N	G	U	P	L	P	M	U	V	A	F
T	U	S	R	U	E	C	A	B	L	M
S	Z	E	T	F	X	S	R	L	A	H
D	I	N	N	E	R	P	A	R	T	Y

One day a man gave a DINNER PARTY. He sent out INVITATIONS but the people he had invited ALL made EXCUSES. The MASTER of the house was ANGRY and told his SERVANTS to go and bring in the POOR, the CRIPPLED, the LAME and the BLIND. "I want my HOUSE to be FULL," he said. "NONE of those invited will TASTE my BANQUET." Luke 14:15-24

3rd SUNDAY AFTER PENTECOST (TRINITY 2)

Year 1 Theme: The Life of the Baptized

Deuteronomy 6:17-end; Romans 6:3-11; John 15:5-11

Ask the children to remember some of Jesus' healing works when he was living as a man in Galilee. Explain how he always felt sorry for people who were sad or ill, and wanted to make them well.

Now tell the story of today's Gospel, referring to a picture if possible.

If the children know of anyone who is ill the whole group can pray for them, imagining Jesus comforting them and asking him to make them well.

Then the children can make this pop-up card. They will need a piece of folded paper, and a semi-circle marked with fold lines; coloured pencils, scissors and glue. Decorate the inside as brightly as possible, and keep the outside plain so that the contrast will be greater when they open the card up.

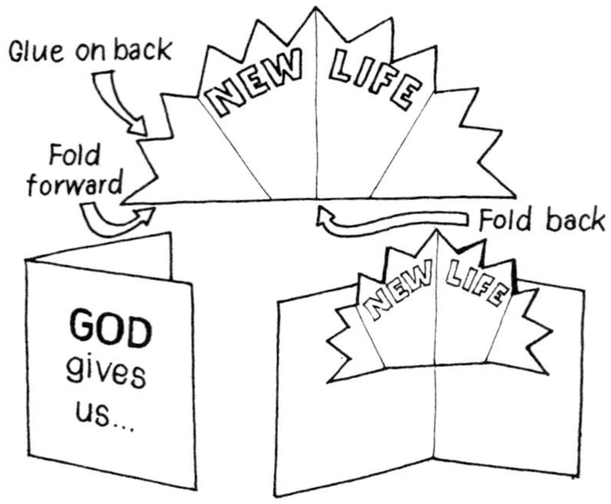
Glue on back
NEW LIFE
Fold forward
Fold back
GOD gives us...
NEW LIFE

Year 2 Theme: The Church's Confidence in Christ

Deuteronomy 8:11-end; Acts 4:8-12; Luke 8:41-end

The children will get a lot from joining in the acting of the Gospel today, along with the adults. If you are not planning to act the Gospel in church, then act it out with the children, after first reading them the story. There are quite a lot of good children's versions of this popular story. Palm Tree's version is called *Becky Gets Better*.

Have a time, too, to praise and thank God for all his gifts to us, and pray for those who are ill, blind, deaf or handicapped in any way. Discuss practical ways the group can help.

Pentecost 3 (1) The Life of the Baptized

IN BAPTISM WE DIE TO SIN AND ARE GIVEN NEW LIFE IN CHRIST.

Romans 6:3-11

Why do we keep this law of God?
bt btgt fnyctf pl Traie ylu Rku ntu df ek sgttukm. Ps bt kwta Rku'f nyb zt bpnn ynbyaf nkko ysetg df.

Deuteronomy 6:20-23

Key to language:

This:	a	b	c	d	e	f	g	i	k	l	m	n	o	p	r	s	t	u	v	w	y	z
means this:	y	w	v	u	t	s	r	p	o	n	m	l	k	i	g	f	e	d	c	b	a	h

Put a O round the words which describe our new life in Christ

vain loving selfish unkind
fulfilled mean generous joyful
thoughtful kind hopeful unfulfilled

Put a X through the words which describe our old life against Christ

Can you translate the answer?

Pentecost 3 (2) The Church's Confidence in Christ

'YOUR FAITH HAS CURED YOU. GO IN PEACE.'

Luke 8:48

Q. Why did Jesus know someone had touched him so as to be healed?

JAIRUS' DAUGHTER HAD DIED
GIVE
MY
GET
EAT
UP
SPIRIT
CHILD

Jesus said to her, " ☐ ▽ ◠ ☐ ". Her ◇ returned ... and he told them to ☁ her something to ✸ Luke 8:40-56

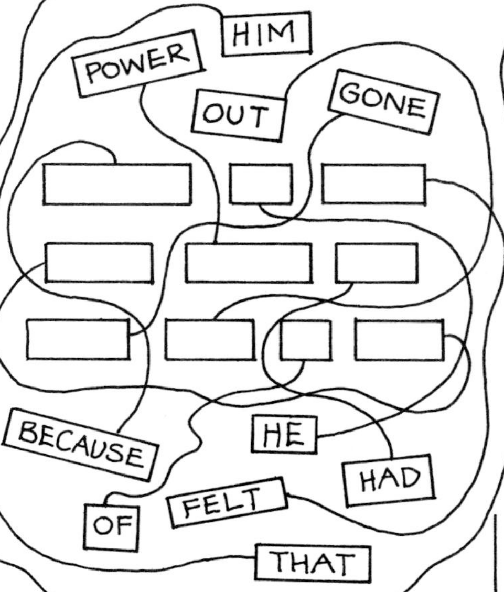

HIM
POWER
OUT
GONE
BECAUSE
HE
HAD
OF
FELT
THAT

4th SUNDAY AFTER PENTECOST (TRINITY 3)

Year 1 Theme: The Freedom of the Sons of God

Deuteronomy 7:6-11; Galatians 3:23-4:7; John 15:12-17

Have on display a selection of things we are given by God which make life possible and enjoyable:

- a glass of water
- lump of coal
- salt
- pictures of a sunrise or sunset
- picture of rain
- plants and flowers

Talk about how much God must love us to give us all these, and many more they can add. Then sing a 'thank you' song.

Now present them with a problem. If they lent a friend one of their toys, and the friend did not use it properly, and broke it, how would they feel? Angry? Upset? What might they do? Take it back? Not lend them anything again? Hit them? (You could write the main points of this discussion up on a board or sheet.)

Then show them some pictures of people spoiling God's world and each other; children quarrelling, being unkind and destructive, people starving while others feast, the aftermath of a bomb explosion etc.

Explain that God sees us all spoiling what he has given us. He feels just as angry and upset, and he could, if he wanted, take the gifts away. As you say this, take away the water, sunlight etc, until the table is bleak and bare.

Why do you think he doesn't do that? Because he loves us so much, even when we are horrid. He hates what we do, sometimes, but he never hates us.

Let the children help put back all the lovely things. If God loves us that much, we must love each other that much.

Year 2 Theme: The Church's Mission to the Individual

Isaiah 63:7-14; Acts 8:26-38; Luke 15:1-10

There are plenty of good versions of these two parables specially for children. Read them one, showing the pictures as you go. Talk about what it feels like to be lost, and then to be found. Remind them that Jesus doesn't want ANY of his 'sheep' to be lost, and we need to learn to love as much as that. Every person is special to God, and that's why we must treat every person as special and precious — even if we don't particularly like the way they behave.

Together make this model of a lost sheep, with the shepherd out looking for it. They can each make a sheep out of card and cotton wool.

Cut out and stick
cotton wool
on card.

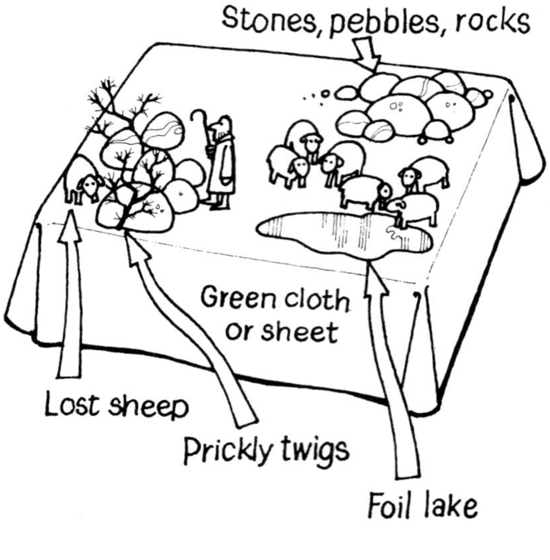
Stones, pebbles, rocks
Green cloth
or sheet
Lost sheep
Prickly twigs
Foil lake

'LOVE ONE ANOTHER AS I HAVE LOVED YOU.'

John 15:12-13

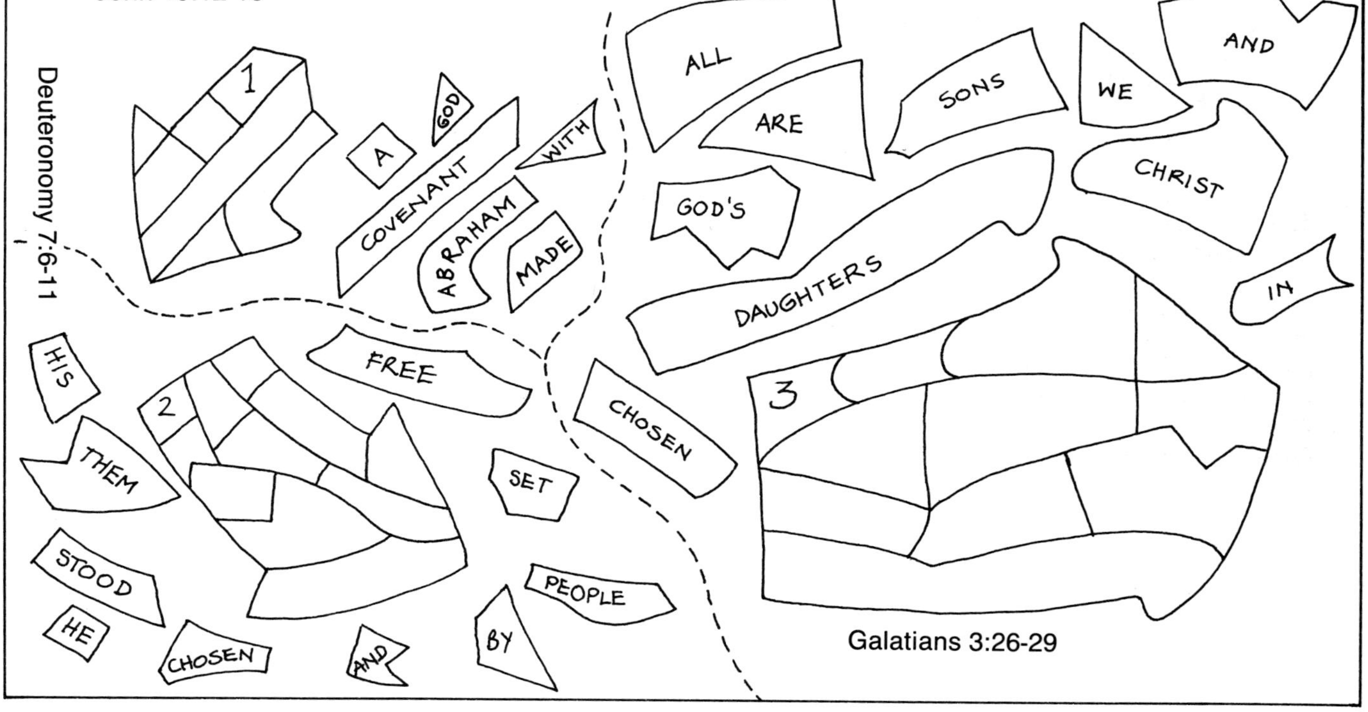
Deuteronomy 7:6-11
1
A
GOD
COVENANT
WITH
ABRAHAM
MADE
ALL
ARE
SONS
WE
AND
GOD'S
CHRIST
DAUGHTERS
IN
HIS
2
FREE
CHOSEN
3
THEM
SET
STOOD
PEOPLE
HE
CHOSEN
AND
BY
Galatians 3:26-29

REJOICE WITH ME FOR I HAVE FOUND MY SHEEP WHICH WAS LOST!

Luke 15:4-7

Help the shepherd find his sheep

baa
Q. Which people are most important to God?
Luke 15:10
A.
V
E
Y
S
!
N
E
R
P
R
O
E

5th SUNDAY AFTER PENTECOST (TRINITY 4)

Year 1 Theme: The New Law

Exodus 20:1-17; Ephesians 5:1-10; Matthew 19:16-26

Have plenty of Bibles available and help the children to find the verses in which the ten commandments are written. It is important that the children are familiar with these and how Moses received them from God. Older children can be encouraged to learn them, with a small prize given to all who manage to do so.

Talk with the children about good manners, and rules they have at home and at school. These are written up on a board or sheet entitled: 'Remember your manners!' They may include:

Keep to the left in the corridor.
Don't speak with your mouth full.
Please and thank you.
Say 'hallo' and 'goodbye'.
Don't interrupt.
Offer food.
Turn T.V. down or off if visitor comes.
Open classroom door to teacher.
Stand at side for people to pass.
Wait your turn in a queue.

Point out that these are ways of caring for others and respecting them. If you love someone, you do this anyway. The rules remind you to act lovingly however you feel about the other person.

Have a lot of supermarket cartons, with the biggest labelled 'Love God with all your heart and soul and mind and strength'. Label the others: 'Friends', 'Money', 'Career', 'Home', 'Holidays', 'Car' etc. Then place the commandments box in the centre of the room and ask the children to help build their lives on it, to make a tall tower. What happens if we take away our base of loving God? Have a volunteer to put out that main box and watch all the rest come tumbling down. You could sing *I want to build my life* (SONL, 95);

Holiday
Car
Money
Home
Friends
Love God with all your heart and soul and mind and strength

Year 2 Theme: The Church's Mission to All Men

Ruth 1:8-17, 22; Acts 11:4-18; Luke 10:1-12

Tell the children how Jesus sent out seventy-two people to go on ahead and prepare others for his coming. Choose some to be the disciples, and get them to take off their socks and shoes. Act out the rest of the Gospel, with the other children being the people who are visited; some are ill and are cured, some make them welcome, and some don't. Show some pictures of Israel so the children can see that Jesus' instructions were practical for travelling light in that climate and terrain.

Gather round in prayer to ask Jesus to show us where he wants us to work for him today and through the week, and give them this prayer to colour and hang up in the bathroom at home and use every morning.

Father, I will give today to you
Show me how to spend it well

Pentecost 5 (1) The New Law

LIVE IN LOVE AS CHRIST LOVED YOU.

Ephesians 5:1-2

1. Have no other God
2. Don't worship idols
3. Never swear using God's name
4. Keep the Sabbath holy
5. Honour your father and mother
6. Don't commit murder
7. Don't commit adultery
8. Don't steal
9. Don't give false evidence
10. Don't covet your neighbour's possessions

The ten Commandments

LOVE GOD	LOVE YOUR NEIGHBOUR

Which go here? Which go here?

WRITE THEM IN

Exodus 20:1-17

"It is easier for a camel to pass through the eye of a needle than for a rich man to enter the kingdom of Heaven."

Can you see why?

Matthew 19:16-26

Pentecost 5 (2) The Church's Mission to All Men

GOD'S GOOD NEWS IS FOR EVERYONE.

Matthew 28:19

A GENTILE is anyone who is not a JEW.
Q. What did Peter find out at Caesarea?

A.

on
Gentiles
and
was
spirit
Jews
both
that
poured
God's
out

Acts 11:4-18

Jesus chose another (18 ÷ 9 =) out (12 × 6 =) people. He sent them out by (14 ÷ 7 =) to heal the sick and tell everyone about God's Kingdom.

Luke 10:1-12

6th SUNDAY AFTER PENTECOST (TRINITY 5)

Theme: The New Man

Year 1

Exodus 24:3-11; Colossians 3:12-17; Luke 15:11-end

The prodigal son is a lovely story to act out. Have a large assortment of dressing up clothes available (curtains, net, lengths of material, old ties and towels etc.)

Tell the children the story, showing pictures of the son:

(a) asking for money;
(b) waving goodbye;
(c) spending it all;
(d) as a pig keeper;
(e) returning home with Father's welcome.

The elder brother can be omitted with young children, as there is plenty for them to grasp without it, and it may make the lesson too complicated.

(f) Angry brother with Father explaining.

Having given parts (plenty can be servants, girl friends and pigs) read out the story bit by bit while the children act it out.

The value of this type of drama is in the involvement, rather than the standard of performance, so suggest what the characters might say as you go along.

Year 2

Micah 6:1-8; Ephesians 4:17-end; Mark 10:46-end

Talk with the children about how difficult it is for blind people to go shopping, cook or even walk along pavements where bikes have been left around. Ask them to shut their eyes for a minute while they try to do an ordinary task like laying a table or putting their shoes and socks on.

Explain how sometimes we can all be 'blind' to other people's needs or to how we are making life difficult for someone. Jesus wants to give us all our sight back.

Now read or tell them the story in today's Gospel, getting a few to mime it as you go. Then help them make these masks to make the point of seeing God's way.

PULL
PULL
SLITS
PULL
I can see!
PULL
I can see!

DRESS YOURSELF IN KINDNESS AND LOVE.

Colossians 3:12-14

LOVE
KINDNESS
PEACE
FORGIVENESS

G	N	I	V	R	A	T	S	F	R
A	T	C	E	Y	B	W	G	A	J
P	B	W	P	N	Y	E	N	T	H
Z	F	P	O	B	I	L	Q	H	T
D	A	S	C	S	E	C	O	E	I
H	Y	L	P	M	X	O	J	R	N
A	E	C	P	E	R	M	G	G	U
F	N	L	K	V	N	E	D	O	H
H	O	M	E	E	L	T	W	M	D
Y	M	S	E	R	V	A	N	T	K

A man had TWO sons. One SON asked his FATHER for his share of MONEY and SPENT every penny. In the end he was STARVING. He went back HOME to ask if his father would EMPLOY him as a SERVANT. But his father RAN to WELCOME him because he was so HAPPY to have him back. GOD welcomes us like this.

Luke 15:11-end

IN CHRIST YOU ARE A NEW PERSON!

2 Corinthians 5:17

mean
miserable
unkind
proud
selfish
kind
generous
happy
gentle

BEFORE AFTER

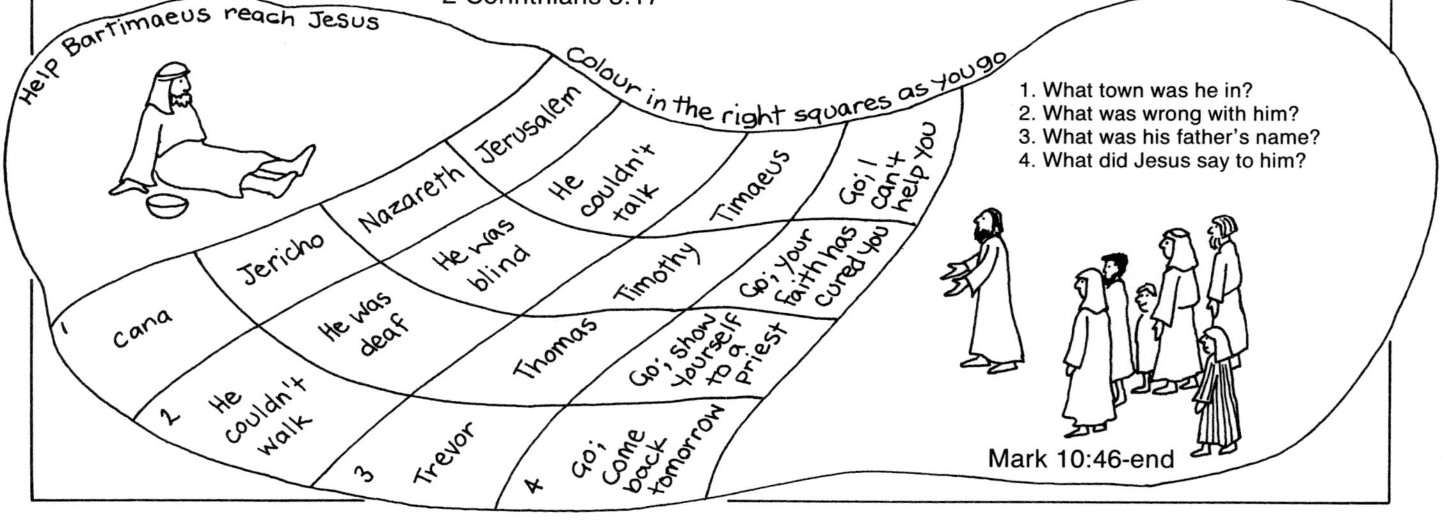
Help Bartimaeus reach Jesus
Colour in the right squares as you go
1 Cana
Jericho
Nazareth
Jerusalem
2 He couldn't walk
He was deaf
He was blind
He couldn't talk
3 Trevor
Thomas
Timothy
Timaeus
4 Go; come back tomorrow
Go; show yourself to a priest
Go; your faith has cured you
Go; I can't help you

1. What town was he in?
2. What was wrong with him?
3. What was his father's name?
4. What did Jesus say to him?

Mark 10:46-end

7th SUNDAY AFTER PENTECOST (TRINITY 6)

Theme: The More Excellent Way

Year 1

Hosea 11:1-9; 1 Corinthians 12:27-13 end; Matthew 18:21-end

Begin by asking them the question Peter asked Jesus — how often do they think they should forgive their brothers and sisters if they keep irritating/breaking toys/teasing etc. It will probably become clear that there is quite a gap between ideals and reality, so help them to be honest!

Then tell them how Peter asked Jesus the same question and how he explained his answer with a story. Tell the story, using different headgear for the various characters, some bills and play money and a pair of handcuffs, or something similar. You can grab hold of a volunteer when the second servant is nearly throttled. If the children have enjoyed an entertaining telling of the story, and been involved in it, they will remember it more.

So having told it and talked about what it says about the way we should behave, let all the children join in an acted version.

Year 2

Deuteronomy 10:12-11:1; Romans 8:1-11; Mark 12:28-34

Beforehand make two simple hand puppets and join them to a piece of stiff card with lengths of string. On the card, stick a sheet of paper with a clearly written script on it. Use different colours for the two characters. Stick the second script on the other side of the card.

Script 1.

Boots Loopy, you must help me.
I need to do a hard sum.
If you stop talking
I can do it.
Loopy O.K. Boots. You do your sum.
I will not talk.
Boots Thank you Loopy.
Now, let me see...
Loopy (sings) La la la la pom pom pom!
Boots Loopy, stop it!
You said you would not talk
so I could do my sum.
Loopy Yes I know I did.
And I have kept my promise.
I was not talking,
I was singing!
Boots Oh, Loopy!!

Script 2.

Boots What are you doing, Loopy?
Loopy I'm sweeping these leaves
for Mr. Tod.
Boots That is kind of you.
Loopy I'm just doing it
to make him think I'm kind.
Then he will give me some sweets.
Boots Wow! That's clever.
I'll sweep too.
He'll never know
we are not really
being kind.

Ask two children to wear the puppets and read the first script so everyone can hear. Was Loopy doing what she was told? Help them to see that in one way she was, yet in another way she wasn't — like when we rush our prayers but have not really talked to God at all.

Ask another two children to read the second script. Mr. Tod told all his friends about how kind Loopy and Boots were. Did they deserve his praise and his sweets? Help them to see that although they had done the sweeping, they had not been honest with Mr. Tod.

Now tell the children about some of the scribes and Pharisees who behaved rather like Loopy and Boots. They did all the right things, down to the very last detail (you could demonstrate all the washing and ritual they went through) but they were not really obeying God's main rule at all.

On a poster, write up God's main Laws, or rules, and see if they can learn them off by heart. Chanting them to a simple melody makes the learning easier, and the Law can be sung to their families in church. *London's burning* works well:

You shall love the Lord your God with
all your mind and all your heart and
all your strength! All your strength!
And love your neighbour, love your neighbour!

LOVE HAS NO LIMIT — IT GOES ON AND ON.

1 Corinthians 13:4-7

How many times must we forgive someone?
3 + 4 =
5 + 5 =
10 + 10 =
10 − 7 =
5 x 3 =
9 + 2 =
9 − 5 =
Add all the boxes up together

GRAND TOTAL
times
at least!

Where is this servant who wouldn't have pity on his fellow servant, even when he himself had been let off a big debt?
JOIN THE DOTS

Matthew 18:21-end

LOVING IS THE BEST WAY TO LIVE.

Mark 12:28-34

Jesus sums up the law like this:
1
the
your God
with
your
and
and
and
+ th
2
your
as
UR

If you live by God's way of LOVE, what would you do about......
this?
this?
this?
this?
this?

8th SUNDAY AFTER PENTECOST (TRINITY 7)

Theme: The Fruit of the Spirit

Year 1

Ezekiel 36:24-28; Galatians 5:16-25; John 15:16-end

Have ready two money boxes or piggy banks and some pretend money (or real, if you wish.) Read the first part of the Gospel.

Explain how Jesus said that following him might be rather expensive, and we'd better decide first whether or not we're prepared to pay the cost before we join him.

What expenses are there in following Jesus? On another 'Christian Expenses' list, write down what we have to spend or give up to be Christians:

- watching television on Sunday mornings;
- telling lies;
- keeping all our sweets to ourselves;
- joining in the unkind teasing; etc.

What do we pay with? Out of the second money box take money shaped cards with:

- kindness;
- love;
- thoughtfulness;
- helpfulness;
- peace-making;
- self-control;
- patience;
- cheerfulness; etc.

It costs a lot, doesn't it? But we couldn't spend it on anything that would make us happier. And remind them that Jesus has spent everything for us — even his life!

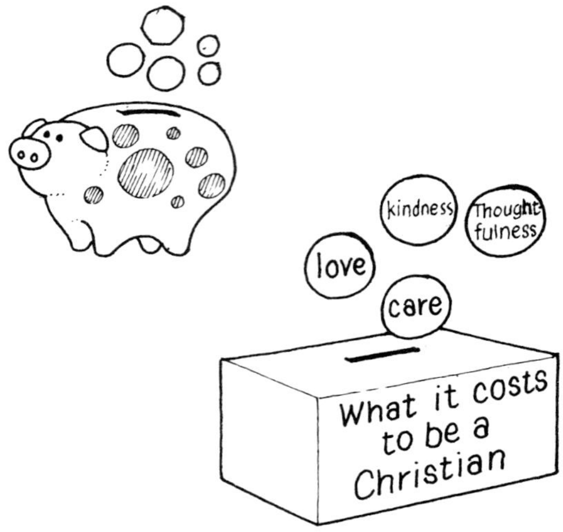
kindness
Thoughtfulness
love
care
What it costs to be a Christian

Give each child a box to decorate and cut out 'coins' to put inside.

Year 2

Ezekiel 37:1-14; 1 Corinthians 12:4-13; Luke 6:27-38

Read or tell the children the teachings in the Gospel today, acting some of them out with different children as you go, and involving them in what they think is the right thing to do in each situation. They may well be surprised at Jesus' advice!

Then talk with them about the sort of thing they find starts them off behaving in an unloving way, and together work out some practical way to avoid the temptation. (Perhaps going out to kick a ball when they feel like kicking a sister; setting a cooking timer to share a toy equally, giving each a set time — until the pinger rings — in which to play; writing a list of daily jobs that need to be done before bed, so things don't get forgotten; asking to sit next to someone in class with whom they are less likely to waste time!)

Give the children paper cups and a pencil. They draw their own face on the side of the cup and punch holes in the bottom. Then, over the grass or a large bowl, pour water from an enormous jug through each child's cup. We are to be channels for God's living Spirit to flow through to the world; we have to work at increasing the flow!

God's living Spirit
WORLD

Pentecost 8 (1) The Fruit of the Spirit

YOU WILL BE KNOWN BY THE FRUIT YOU BEAR.

Matthew 7:18-20

The fruits of the Spirit are
Galatians 5:16-25
JOY
LOVE
PEACE
PATIENCE
KINDNESS
GOODNESS
TRUSTFULNESS
GENTLENESS
SELF-CONTROL
Draw a tree for them to grow on
Put your own name on the tree

NOW COLOUR IT ALL IN!

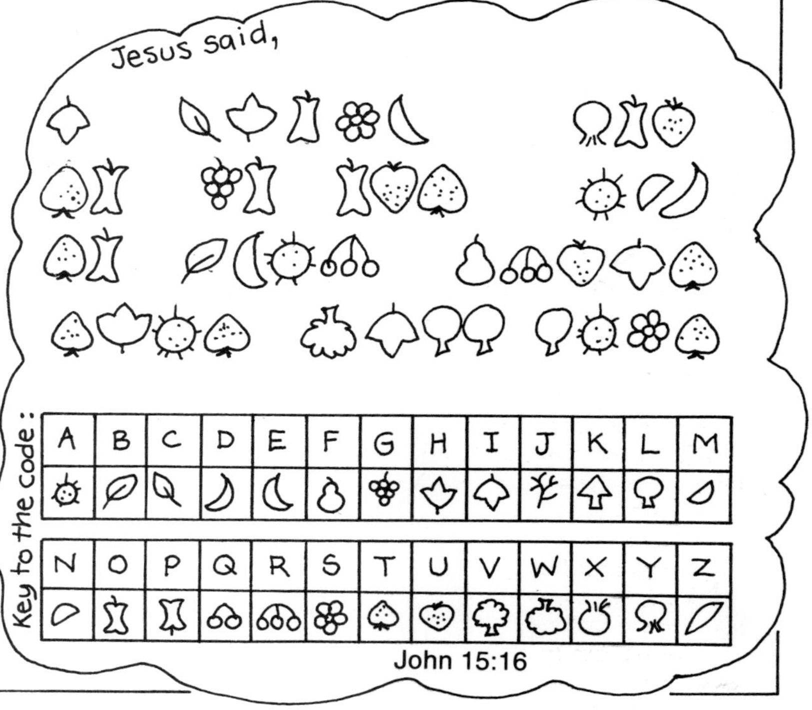

Jesus said,
Key to the code:
A B C D E F G H I J K L M
N O P Q R S T U V W X Y Z

John 15:16

Pentecost 8 (2) The Fruit of the Spirit

LOVE YOUR ENEMIES; DO GOOD TO THOSE WHO HATE YOU.

Luke 6:27-38

Can you see God's message? Colour it in, so it shows up clearly

Ezekiel 37:1-14

When God lives in us, it shows, and turns the world upside down!
then willingly go 2 miles
If someone curses you,
treat them with kindness and pray for them
If a man takes your coat,
you must not curse them back. Bless them instead
If you are forced to go one mile
If someone treats you spitefully,
offer him your shirt as well!
MATCH THE PATCH

9th SUNDAY AFTER PENTECOST (TRINITY 8)

Theme: The Whole Armour of God

Year 1

Joshua 1:1-9; Ephesians 6:10-20; John 17:11b-19

Bring along a selection of protective clothing, such as a cagoule, umbrella and over-trousers; crash helmet, leather jacket and strong boots; white coat and clinical mask; soldier's helmet, sword and shield. Put them on in turn, getting the children to help and suggest what each outfit protects you against. They may be able to think of some other protective clothing, too.

Now read or tell them what Paul says about how we can protect ourselves against evil. Go through the list again, this time putting labels on each item as you dress one child up in full armour. (If you can't get hold of a dressing up set of Roman armour, make a set from cardboard, using the pattern shown.) Then give each child a picture of a person, and the different items of spiritual armour, each labelled, which they colour and fix on.

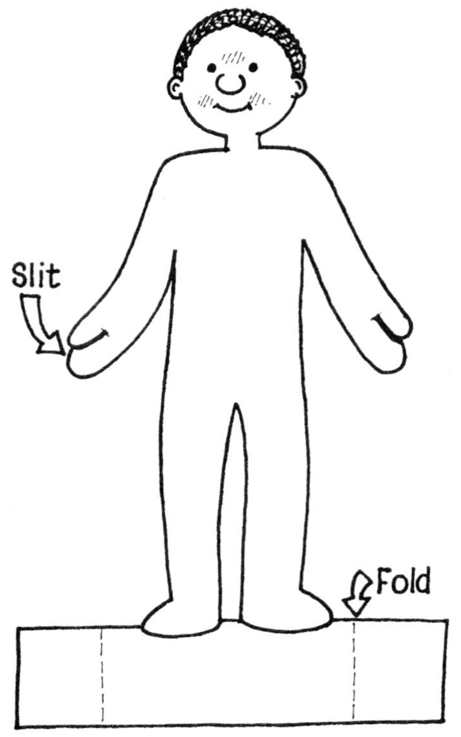

Slit
Fold

Salvation
God's word
Peace
Peace
Faith
Righteousness
Truth

Year 2

1 Samuel 17:37-50; 2 Corinthians 6:3-10; Mark 9:14-29

This is a favourite story with children and there are many excellent versions of it with pictures to use. Palm Tree also publish a giant picture of David and Goliath for a whole group of children to work on. Alternatively, give the children modelling clay to make their own David and Goliath. They can set their models in a boxed landscape.

Crumpled newspaper under green paper for the hill
David trusts in God

PUT ON THE WHOLE ARMOUR OF GOD.

Ephesians 6:10-20

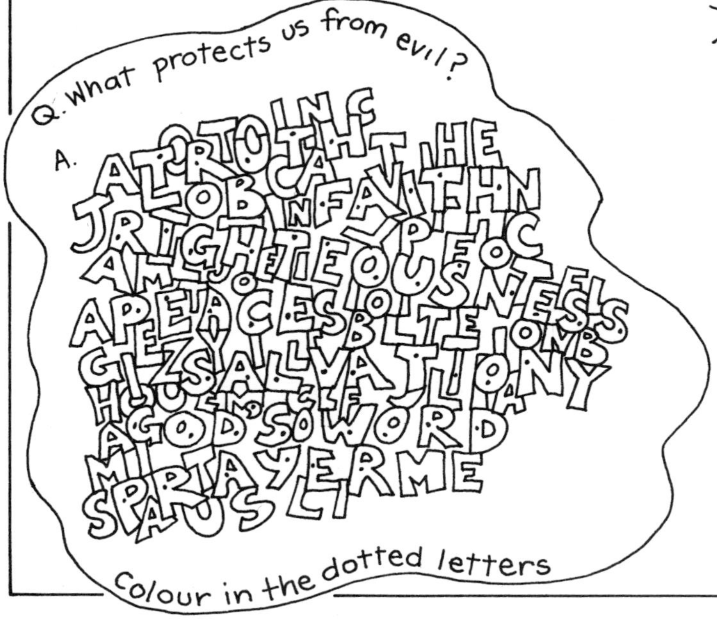
Q. What protects us from evil?
A.
Colour in the dotted letters

BODUT
RIPDE
RGEDE
ISLE
IPEDSAR
ARTHED
REFA
Can you unjumble the arrows that attack us?

GOD'S POWER MAKES THE IMPOSSIBLE HAPPEN!

Mark 9:14-29

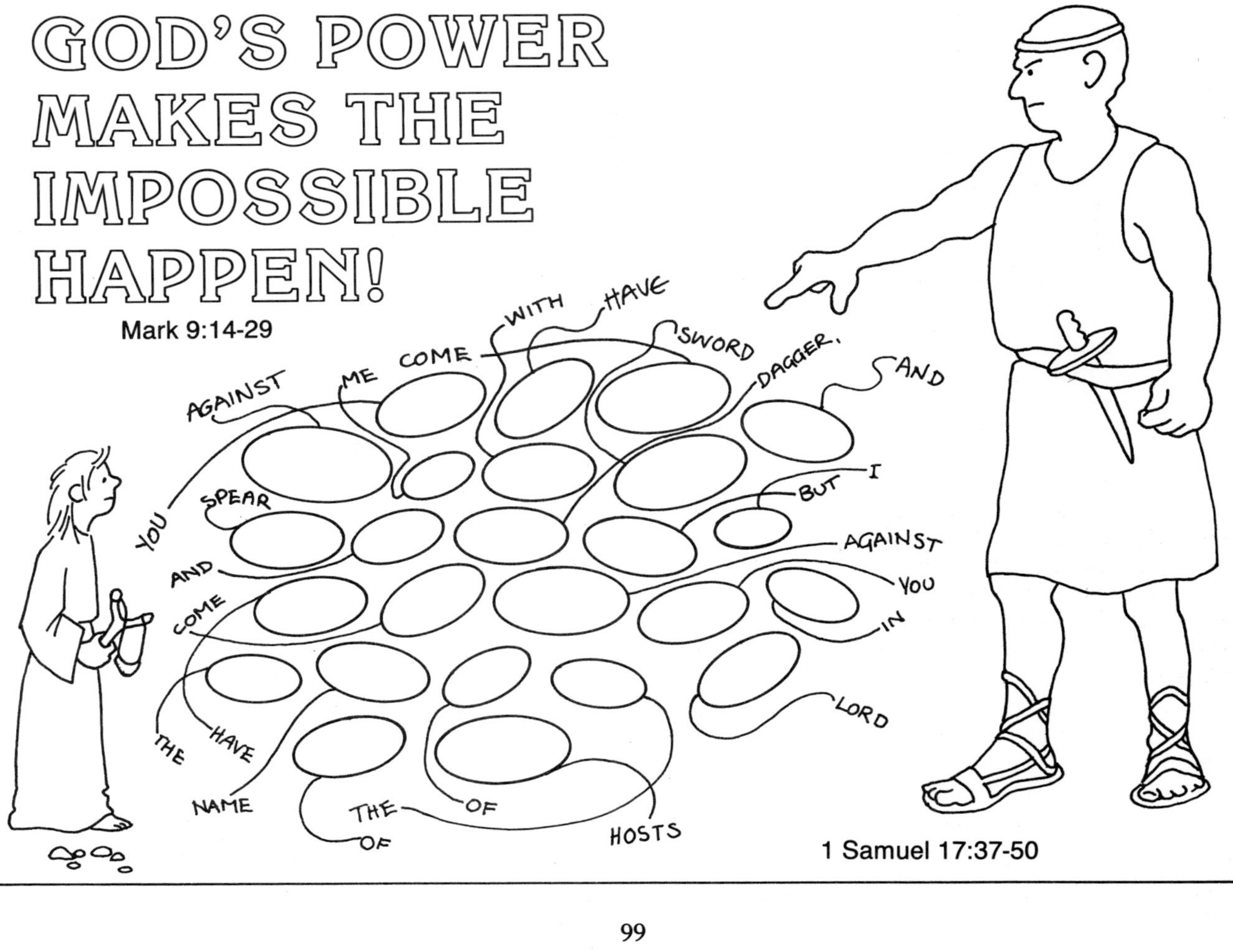
YOU
AGAINST
ME
COME
WITH
HAVE
SWORD
DAGGER,
AND
SPEAR
AND
COME
BUT
I
AGAINST
YOU
IN
THE
HAVE
NAME
THE
OF
OF
HOSTS
LORD

1 Samuel 17:37-50

10th SUNDAY AFTER PENTECOST (TRINITY 9)

Theme: The Mind of Christ

Year 1

Job 42:1-6; Philippians 2:1-11; John 13:1-15

Have a display of all kinds of interesting and lovely things in God's world, and give the children some time to examine them, enjoy them and find out about them. (Have magnifying glasses handy, and direct their attention to colours, textures, behaviour etc.)

Talk together about the wonderful world, which shows us something about God, just as the pictures we paint show others something about us. Sing some praise songs, and then tell them how Jesus, in spite of all his greatness, acts like a servant. Explain how the servants of that time washed people's feet because it was a hot, dusty country. Then wash one or two children's feet to show them. What servant jobs can they do cheerfully, to follow Jesus' example? Arrange for them to help with clearing up the coffee cups after church, or doing some other very dull job in a happy, friendly way as an act of praise.

Year 2

1 Samuel 24:9-17 (or 1-17); Galatians 6:1-10; Luke 7:36-end

Tell the story Jesus told Simon, using the children to help you. First choose a postman, and give him a bag and badge (or hat) with two bills to deliver.

'One morning the postman delivered a letter to Sam Butcher. (Postman gives one bill to him.) Sam opened it (let him open it and show everyone) and inside was a bill for £5.

How do you think Sam felt? A bit fed up/miserable? "At least it's not *too* big a bill," he thought. "I'll have to go without all my sweets this week."

Then the postman delivered a letter to Robert South. (He delivers it.) Robert opened it and looked inside. It was a bill for £5000!

How do you think Robert felt? He was very worried and sad, because he didn't have much money at all. "Oh dear," he thought, "I'll *never* manage to pay this. Not unless I sell my house — and then where could I live?"

He felt worried and sad all day. He hardly slept that night, for thinking about the way he couldn't pay that huge bill. Perhaps he would be sent to prison, even.

Next morning the postman delivered another letter to Sam and another to Robert. They opened them, rather nervously. Inside was an important looking letter. It said (let the children read it our together)

Dear Sir,
I am going to let you off.
You need not pay me
the money after all.
Best wishes,
Tom Smith (Manager)

Well, how do you think they felt? Happy/delighted/relieved? They felt very relieved and happy. Sam was glad he could buy some sweets as usual.

But who do you think felt most thankful? It was Robert! He had been so worried and sad, and it was as if a great heavy weight was lifted off him. He ran out to Tom Smith's office to thank him straight away. He would never forget Tom's kindness.'

Explain that Jesus is rather like Tom Smith, and we are like Sam and Robert. When we do something wrong or unkind it is like being in debt. When we are forgiven, our debt is paid, and we feel happy and relieved again. Let the children make these cards to remind them.

I.O.U.
££££

YOUR SINS
ARE FORGIVEN..
GO IN PEACE!

Pentecost 10 (1) The Mind of Christ

LET THE MIND OF CHRIST BE IN YOU IN THE WAY YOU THINK AND LIVE.

Philippians 2:1-11

T	B	H	T	C	V	D	S	R	F
G	R	E	A	T	Q	D	H	T	O
X	E	E	W	C	O	I	U	N	L
F	B	Z	A	G	U	S	M	A	L
B	P	N	E	T	H	C	I	V	O
Y	E	V	A	O	D	I	L	R	W
H	O	E	W	F	M	P	I	E	E
L	J	E	S	U	S	L	T	S	R
F	D	L	O	R	D	E	Y	E	S
O	J	G	D	E	H	S	A	W	T

John 13:1-15

When Jesus WASHED the FEET of his DISCIPLES, he SHOWED them how they were to TREAT one another. JESUS was their LORD, but he acted as their SERVANT. So if his FOLLOWERS want to be GREAT in GOD'S EYES they must look after one another with LOVE and HUMILITY.

Pentecost 10 (2) The Mind of Christ

ACT LIKE CHRIST, WITH FORGIVENESS AND CARING LOVE.

Galatians 6:1-5

Luke 7:36-end

1 Samuel 24:1-7

Two men are let off a debt. One owed 50p the other £500. Which one will be most grateful?
YES
NO
If you're forgiven a lot, you'll love God a lot
NO
King Saul has been looking for David to kill him. Now David has the chance to kill Saul. What does he do?
Kills Saul in revenge
Lets Saul go away without knowing his danger
Cuts off a bit of Saul's cloak but does no harm to Saul

11th SUNDAY AFTER PENTECOST (TRINITY 10)

Theme: The Serving Community

Year 1

Isaiah 42:1-7; 2 Corinthians 4:1-10; John 13:31-35

Collect some pictures of missionary work, both at home and abroad, and discuss with the children what the needs are and how they are being met. Point out that the missionaries are telling people about the God of love not only by what they say but also how they behave and what they do.

Discuss with them the kind of things they would like others to know about their special friend, Jesus — who he was, how he helps them and what he is like.

Write down their words on coloured paper which they can illustrate, and then staple the whole lot together to make a book. If possible have it duplicated and used as an aid in mission; children's straightforward and trusting faith is a great witness.

GOD made the world
When we are sorry he forgives us
hen he orgives me feel very happy
Jesus understands how I feel
When he died it must have hurt a lot
elps me remember to be kind
Jesus made lots of people better
When I feel scared he helps me be brave
WOOF
always there when I need him

Year 2

1 Chronicles 29:1-9; Philippians 1:1-11; Matthew 20:1-16

First discuss with the children what work there is in a vineyard, such as grape picking, treading the grapes, weeding, pruning etc. Everyone can act out each job.

Without telling the story first, begin acting it out, with one child taking the part of the landowner. Narrate it simply, and split the other children into five groups (or fewer if numbers are small) to be the workers hanging around the market place. Make sure that the first group is quite clear about how much money they will earn — let them shake hands during the deal. And make much of those who work hard during the hot blistering day.

When it comes to the giving out of wages, see how the children react to the amount the last workers are given, but don't give away the surprise. When the first workers receive their wages it will be interesting to see how they take it, and it should give rise to some lively discussion on what is fair and what is generous.

Bring out two points:

1. Jesus never gives up looking for us in the market place to see if we'd like to work for him.
2. If we do decide to give him our time and energy, then even if we were a long while getting there, Jesus will welcome us and we shall not lose the good reward at the end.

Help the children make a model of a vineyard and workers out of plasticine, and assorted boxes, paper, string, pipecleaners etc.

PEOPLE WILL KNOW YOU ARE MY FRIENDS BY THE WAY YOU LOVE ONE ANOTHER.

John 13:34-35

2 Corinthians 4:7-8

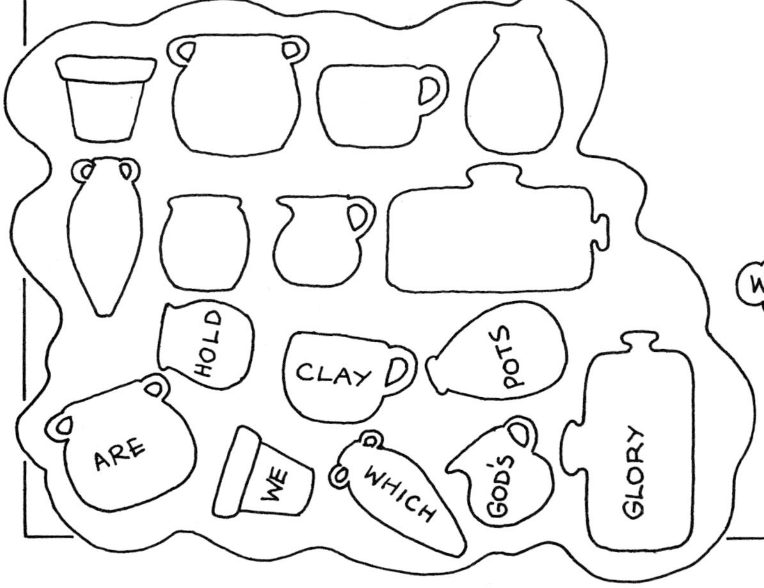

HOLD
CLAY
POTS
ARE
WE
WHICH
GOD'S
GLORY

Why?
Because....
GOD
+E

ENCOURAGE ONE ANOTHER AS YOU WORK TOGETHER.

Philippians 1:1-11

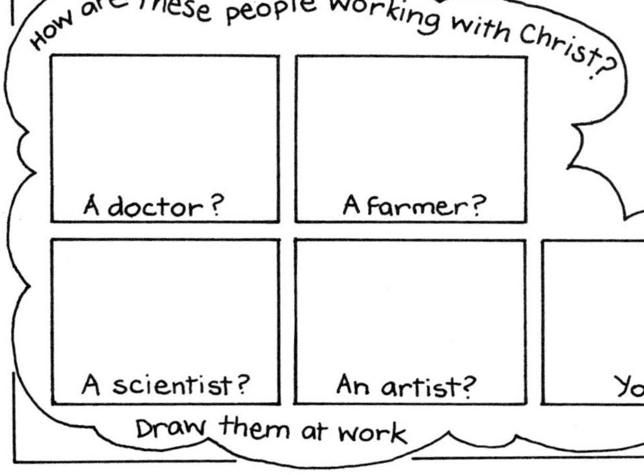

How are these people working with Christ?
A doctor?
A farmer?
A scientist?
An artist?
You?
Draw them at work

Who is willing to give to the Lord today?
M _ _ _ _ _
B _ _ _ _ _
J _ _ _ _ _
S _ _ _ _ _
I _ _ _
G _ _ _
Solomon is collecting materials for building a beautiful temple. What are the people bringing?

1 Chronicles 29:6-9

12th SUNDAY AFTER PENTECOST (TRINITY 11)

Theme: The Witnessing Community

Year 1

Isaiah 49:1-6; 2 Corinthians 5:14-6:2; John 17:20-end

Today offers a good opportunity to learn about some of the famous 'witnesses' to God's love. Make sure they know what it means to witness something — their real experience of something proves its truth, as in car accidents or in court.

Saints are people who have witnessed to God's love; their lives have shown others what God's love is like. The parish church's patron saint will probably be a well-known figure; include a variety of others, such as:

Francis of Assisi	Clare
Paul	Margaret of Scotland
Peter	Catherine
Dunstan	Joan of Arc

or any others whose lives are exciting to read about. Have information, books and pictures available, and split the children into small groups to make a display about one particular saint. They can then share their work with the others, and put the whole exhibition up in church entitled: 'You are the light of the world'. 'Let your light shine'.

Year 2

Micah 4:1-5; Acts 17:22-end; Matthew 5:13-16

Bring along the following:
- some sea salt;
- something preserved in brine (e.g. frankfurters);
- some small cubes of cheese (enough for one each)
- a candle;
- a large metal saucepan.

First sprinkle some grains of salt on a plate and talk about what it is (they can taste it if they like). Explain how it was used to keep food before anyone had freezers and fridges. Sometimes it is still used like that (give examples) and in hotter countries it is still used to preserve meat and fish. See if they can taste the saltiness in cheese — the salt keeps it fresh.

Now read what Jesus said about us being salt. Discuss with them what this means for us: how can we be salt in the world? It may be helpful to have this question on a board or sheet of paper, and jot down their ideas to keep track of them.

Then light the candle, and talk about useful lights such as torches, street lamps, car lights etc. Cover the light with the saucepan, and help them see how silly this is, if we want to light the room.

Now read the second part of today's Gospel and jot down ideas under a second question: how can we be the light of the world?

Sing *I'm gonna let my little light shine* and help the children to make these Chinese lanterns from stiff paper. They can carry these into church.

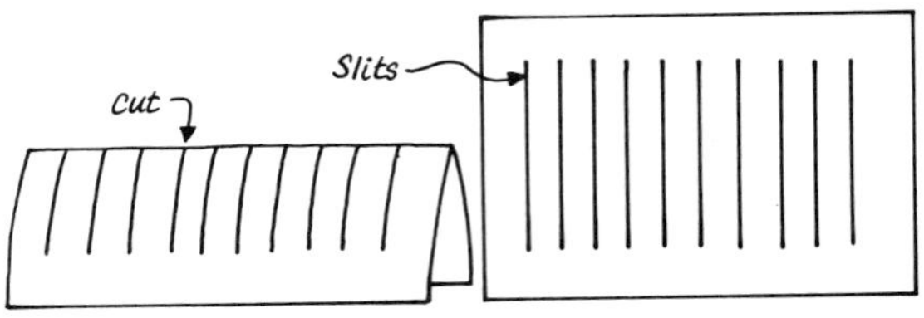
Slits
Cut

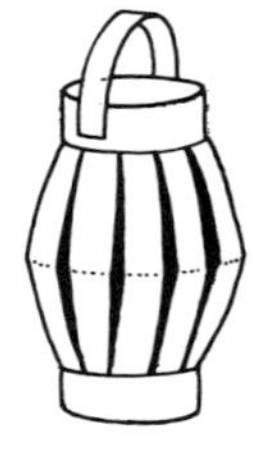

Pentecost 12 (1) The Witnessing Community

YOU WILL BE MY WITNESSES THROUGHOUT THE WORLD

John 17:20-21

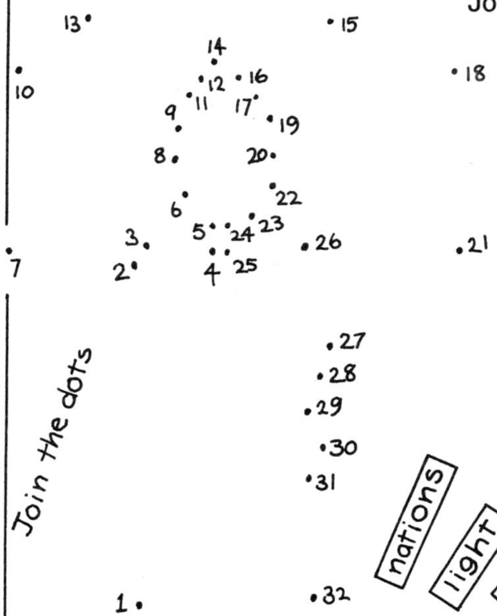

13 15 14 12 16 18 10 9 11 17 19 8 20 6 22 5 24 23 3 26 21 7 2 4 25 27 28 29 30 31 1 32

Join the dots

nations light make

"I will [ ] you a [ ] to the [ ]" says the Lord. (Isaiah 49:6)

What had the apostles seen Jesus doing?

circle the right ones

- telling lies
- making the blind see
- dying and being alive again
- healing lepers
- leading a revolt
- teaching the crowds
- Making lots of money

How can we witness to God's saving love?

circle the right ones, and add your own.

- being moody
- standing up against evil
- letting people do evil if they want
- putting prayer into action
- forgiving quickly
- not getting involved

Pentecost 12 (2) The Witnessing Community

WE WILL WALK IN THE NAME OF THE LORD OUR GOD!

Micah 4:5

'Let your life shine to show God's glory!'

yellow
orange
red
red
red
red
red
red
red

Who is the God we worship?

- The one who made mountains?
- The one who made the sea?
- The one who made the whole universe?

Where is the God we worship?

- very close – we live and move in him
- on a holy mountain?
- far away above the sky

How do we know what God is like?

- because when we pray we start behaving like him
- because we can see him in Jesus
- because the world he made shows us his character

COLOUR THE TRUE SHAPES

Acts 17:24-28

13th SUNDAY AFTER PENTECOST (TRINITY 12)

Theme: The Suffering Community

Year 1

Isaiah 50:4-9a; Acts 7:54-8:1; John 16:1-11

Jesus was not just a good man but actually the Son of God. Draw a large cross as the sign of Jesus, in the centre of a sheet of paper. The prophets in the Old Testament spoke about what Jesus would be like and what he would do. Now draw in (or stick on) some people on the left side of the cross, looking towards it. Write in some speech balloons with quotations referring to the Christ:

Daniel 7:13-14
I saw... there came one like a son of man... and to him was given dominion and glory and kingdom.
Micah 5:2
From you, Bethlehem, shall come a ruler... who shall feed his flock in the strength of the Lord.
Isaiah 60:3
Kings shall come to the brightness of your rising.
Isaiah 53:5
He was wounded for our wrongdoing.

and discuss with the children how these fit in with Jesus' life. They will see that his suffering for us is mentioned; the cross is part of the loving.

Jesus told his friends that if they wanted to follow him they would have to be prepared to suffer as well. Ask the children to colour and cut out pictures of themselves to stick on the right side of the cross, looking towards it.

Before
CHRIST
After

Year 2

Jeremiah 20:7-11a; Acts 20:17-35; Matthew 10:16-22

Read today's Gospel — God's work sounds rather frightening, but he promises to come with us and tell us what to say. Jesus doesn't pretend it will be easy, but he still asks us to stay with him for the good of our world. What will we do?

Help them make this moving picture.

GLUE FLAP
FOLD
FOLD
FOLD
GLUE FLAP

Do you want to go away?
I want to stay with you, Jesus!

JESUS HAD TO SUFFER SO AS TO SET US FREE.

John 16:1-11

All these people have suffered for their faith
Join the shapes to see who's who

- Catherine
- live in the poorest slums in Calcutta so as to look after the dying
- Terry Waite
- went to live and work among lepers, and died of leprosy
- Dietrich Bonhoeffer
- Father Damien
- was imprisoned and tortured for teaching others about Jesus
- Mother Teresa and her companions
- is being held hostage for working to get others free
- was put to death for being a Christian

DANGER

You may well have to suffer if you give your life for Christ to use

TER
DO
U
O
E
N
FR + ENED
4
THE
SW
L
E
I
D
WITH
U.

I AM SENDING YOU OUT AS SHEEP AMONG WOLVES.

Matthew 10:16-22

suppose you are asked to tell someone why you are a Christian.....

Key to the code:
A B C D E G H I K L N O R S T U V W Y

Sheep
pen

Can you get through without the wolves getting you?

14th SUNDAY AFTER PENTECOST (TRINITY 13)

Theme: The Family

Year 1

Proverbs 31:10-end; Ephesians 5:25-6:4; Mark 10:2-16

Bring along a selection of toy farmyard and zoo animals and people and let the children group them into families of mother, father and baby. Or you could use a Happy Families set of cards to sort into families.

Now read the children the story of creation; *Palm Tree Bible Stories* has a version called *God makes the world*. They will see how God started the family idea right at the beginning of humanity's creation. Show them some wedding pictures and point out that it is God who joins the couple in marriage.

Using card tubes, scraps of net and other material, colour pens and glue, help them make a bride and bridegroom holding hands.

a
b
a
b

Year 2

Genesis 45:1-15; Ephesians 3:14-end; Luke 11:1-13

Talk with the children about asking. Suppose they would like a friend round to play or some help with a tricky model they are building, what would they do? Ask Mummy and Daddy, and if they can help, they will. It's no good just thinking to ourselves, 'If only I could have my friend to play.' We have to ask, and then we've got a good chance of our hopes coming true. (At this stage show the first sign: 'Ask and you will receive.') Point out that it's the same with our heavenly Father; it's no good just thinking to ourselves, 'If only I didn't get bad-tempered so often!' or 'If only I wasn't so scared of owning up!' But if we ASK our heavenly Father, he will help us to change!

Have ready hidden an object in the room. Tell the children something is hidden. How can they find it? By looking! (Let them hunt till they find it. Then show the second sign: 'Seek and you will find.') Point out that in the same way we will never find out about Jesus, or ourselves or other people unless we get up and make an effort to find out, by reading the Bible, asking people, thinking and being aware.

Show a picture of a front door. How can you get someone to open it? By knocking or ringing the bell — no one will answer unless you do! (Show third sign: 'Knock and the door will be opened to you.') It is the same with God, our Father. He is there, alive, strong and he likes us — in fact, he loves us! But he will never push into our lives; if we want his help, or if we want to know about his way of living, we must ASK, SEEK and KNOCK at the door.

Let three groups colour and decorate the three signs, to be put in church where everyone can see them. Then join in prayer together, encouraging the children to add their prayers too.

ASK
AND YOU WILL RECEIVE
SEEK
AND YOU WILL FIND

KNOCK

Pentecost 14 (1) The Family

'LET THE CHILDREN COME TO ME AND DON'T TRY TO STOP THEM'.

Mark 10:13-16

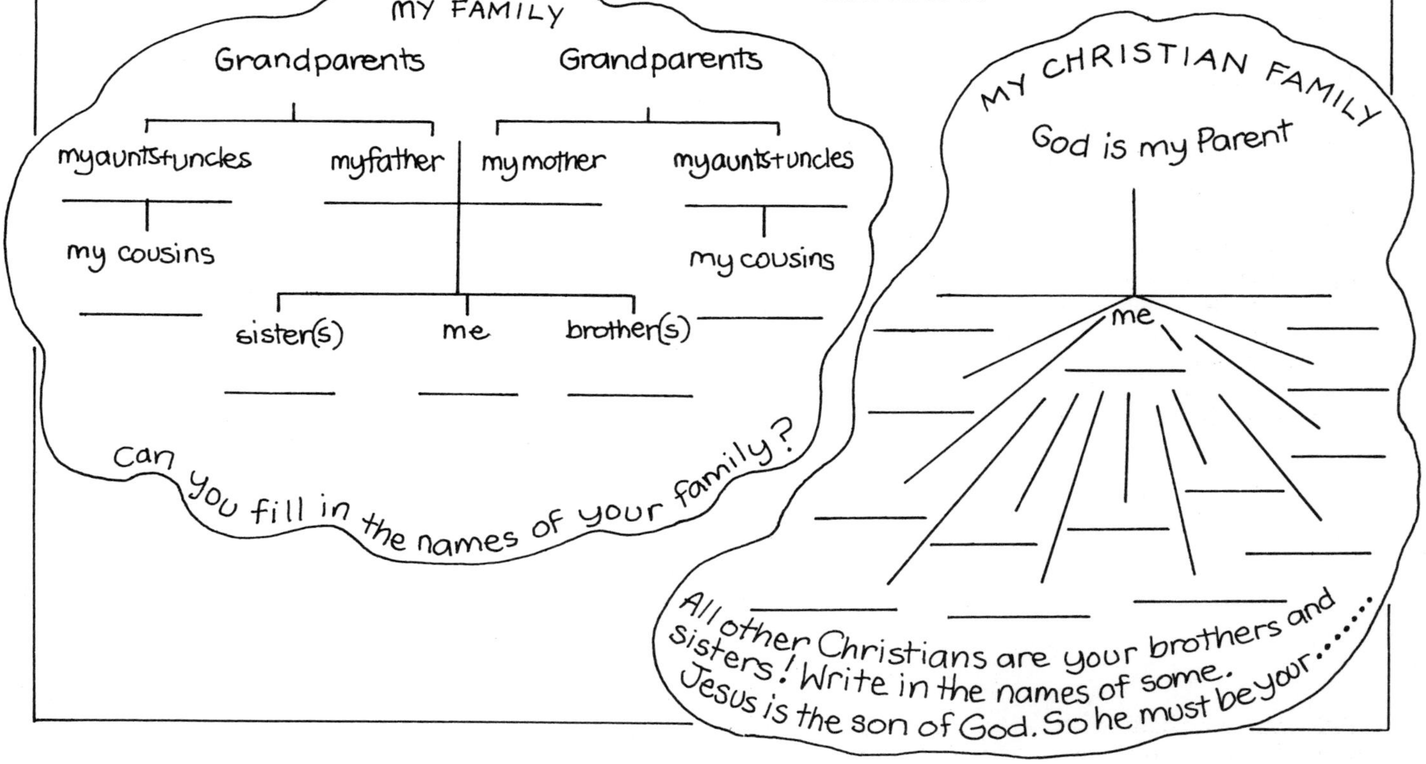

MY FAMILY
Grandparents
Grandparents
my aunts+uncles
my father
my mother
my aunts+uncles
my cousins
my cousins
sister(s)
me
brother(s)
Can you fill in the names of your family?
MY CHRISTIAN FAMILY
God is my Parent
me
All other Christians are your brothers and sisters! Write in the names of some.
Jesus is the son of God. So he must be your......

Pentecost 14 (2) The Family

YOUR HEAVENLY FATHER KNOWS YOUR NEEDS.

Luke 11:9-13

AND YOU WILL RECEIVE
AND THE DOOR WILL BE OPENED
AND YOU WILL FIND
ASK
SEEK
KNOCK

Draw in the people in your own family and write their names under their pictures. God is the Father of us all. We are all his _ _ _ _ _ _ _ _ _ _ _ .

Ephesians 3:14-end

15th SUNDAY AFTER PENTECOST (TRINITY 14)

Theme: Those in Authority

Year 1

Isaiah 45:1-7; Romans 13:1-7; Matthew 22:15-22

Jesus' lifetime can sometimes appear like a fairy tale to children, and today's Gospel provides a good opportunity to fasten it firmly in history, with the Romans.

Have a book on the Romans (the local library will have some available) and show the children how they lived, and which countries they ruled. Point out that the people of those countries (Britain as well as Israel) disliked paying taxes to foreign rulers. Also show the children some pictures of Roman coins, and some of our own coins to see whose head is on those.

Now tell the story of the Pharisees' clever question, pointing out how difficult it was for Jesus to answer without getting into deep trouble, either with his people or the Romans. Tell them how Jesus answered, and have this answer written out clearly ready to display: 'Give back to Caesar what belongs to Caesar — give back to God what belongs to God.' They can all say this together, or even learn it for next week.

What does belong to God, that we can give him back?

- our time
- our life
- our thanks
- our praise. . . *ourselves!*

Sing *Father, you have given us a bright new day* (MWTP, 105) or *The clock tells the story of time God gives us* (MWTP, 16).

Year 2

1 Kings 3:4-15; 1 Timothy 2:1-7; Matthew 14:1-12

Prepare three large posters each with four sheets of paper staples at the top, like this:

1. Is it right to go to Church?...
2. ...even if your friend invites you to play instead?
3. ...even if you have homework to do?
4. ...even if your mother breaks her ankle and needs help?
1. Is it right to read your Bible?..
2. ...even if Someone says you are silly?..
3. ...even if you have your cat to feed?...
4. ...even if it is time to go to School?...
1. Is it right to pray?...
2. ...even if you are not in Church?...
3. ...even if you are in a hurry?...
4. ...even if you are in a car crash?...

Look together at the one about going to church. The answer to the first two questions is going to be YES; the third circumstance is more difficult. In the end the answer should still be YES, as long as they plan to rearrange other activities that day to make sure the necessary jobs get done as well. The fourth circumstance helps the children explore the kind of situation when a good rule has to be broken in order to do God's will. Obeying God's law of love must always take precedence.

Next, deal with the question of Bible reading in the same way, and finally the question of prayer. This one will be different, because there is no time at all when keeping in touch with God is wrong; in fact, the more difficult the situation, the closer we cling!

After this discussion, show the children a picture of Jesus healing the man with the withered arm. Was it a good thing he was doing? Tell or read how the Pharisees reacted and how Jesus showed that even the best rules are not as important as living life in God's loving way.

Pentecost 15 (1) Those in Authority

GIVE TO CAESAR WHAT BELONGS TO CAESAR; GIVE TO GOD WHAT BELONGS TO GOD.

Matthew 22:15-22

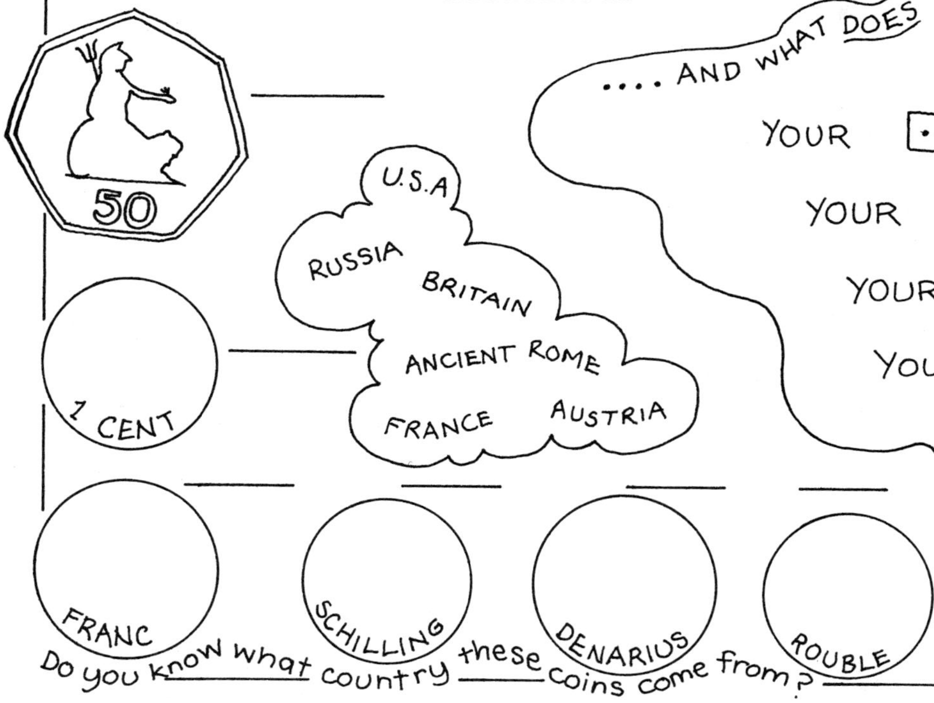
50
U.S.A
RUSSIA
BRITAIN
ANCIENT ROME
FRANCE
AUSTRIA
1 CENT
FRANC
SCHILLING
DENARIUS
ROUBLE
Do you know what country these coins come from?

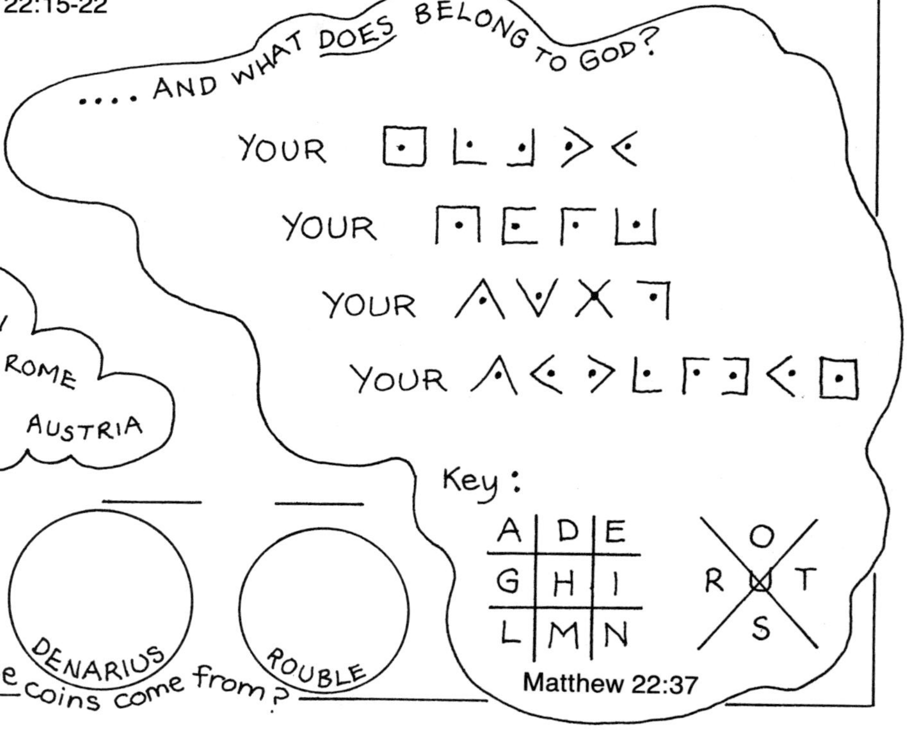
.... AND WHAT DOES BELONG TO GOD?
YOUR
YOUR
YOUR
YOUR
Key:
A D E
G H I
L M N
O
R U T
S
Matthew 22:37

Pentecost 15 (2) Those in Authority

PRAY FOR ALL LEADERS, THAT THEY MAY RULE WISELY.

1 Timothy 2:1-7

King Solomon was young, and knew his job would not be easy. What did he ask God to give him?

POWER
RICHES
WISDOM
HAPPINESS
HEALTH
(colour in the dotted letters)

God was so glad he asked for this, that he gave him the other things as well!

1 Kings 3:4-15

"Let your Kingdom come." What do we mean?

IN
OF
LET
GOD
RULE
BE
US
CHARGE
GOD
OUR
LET
WORLD

16th SUNDAY AFTER PENTECOST (TRINITY 15)

Theme: The Neighbour

Year 2

Leviticus 19:9-18; Romans 12:9-end; Luke 10:25-37

The Good Samaritan is an excellent story for the children to act out, but it needs to be clearly explained first.

If the priest and the Levite touched a dead man they would be considered 'unclean' by the Law. The man looked dead, so they passed by, pretending they hadn't noticed.

The Samaritan came from another country so it was extra strange for him to bother with the man. But because he saw the man needed help he felt sorry for him, and helped him as best he could.

There are several book versions of the story which can be used. Give the children lots of help with what to do and say, setting out the room first with a road, an inn, Jerusalem and Jericho. Have strips of material for bandages and some pretend ointment in a small pot, some play money in a bag and some plastic cups for the people at the inn.

Year 2

Deuteronomy 15:7-11; 1 John 4:15-end; Luke 16:19-end

Continuing our practical involvement with those in need, make a display board of something like the Clean Water project, or Famine relief, tree planting and mud stoves or a sponsored village.

Supply bright background paper and pictures from newspapers and magazines. Many of the relief organisations are happy to supply excellent material: a selection of addresses is below.

Begin the session with a song of thanks.

Then tell the story that Jesus told about the rich man and Lazarus, and follow up last week's activities for helping before arranging this week's display.

Make it as clear as possible by headings, questions and maps. Coloured wool pinned between areas of the map and relevant information may be helpful.

Display the board where the rest of the congregation can see it, possibly bringing it in at the offertory.

Useful Addresses

Action Aid, 208 Upper Street, London N1 1RZ
Christian Aid, P.O. Box 1, London SW9 8BH
Oxfam, 274 Banbury Road, Oxford OX2 7DZ
Traidcraft, Kingsway, Gateshead NE11 0NE
U.S.P.G., Partnership House, 157 Waterloo Road, London SE1 8XA
V.S.O., 9 Belgrave Square, London SW1X 8PW

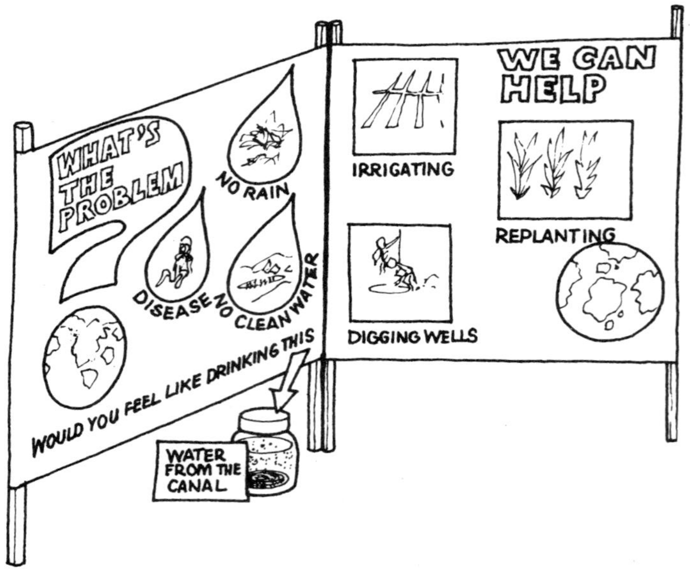
WHAT'S THE PROBLEM
NO RAIN
DISEASE
NO CLEAN WATER
WOULD YOU FEEL LIKE DRINKING THIS
WATER FROM THE CANAL
WE CAN HELP
IRRIGATING
REPLANTING
DIGGING WELLS

Pentecost 16 (1) The Neighbour

OVERCOME EVIL WITH GOOD.

Romans 12:9-end

HOW?
If someone hates you
If your enemy is thirsty
If your enemy is hungry
hate what is evil;
love him and forgive him
give her a drink
hold tight to what is good
....feed him

Y	R	R	O	S	D	D	A	F	W
A	B	T	S	E	I	R	P	O	D
I	D	F	G	A	E	A	U	R	L
R	S	G	P	C	S	N	P	E	O
A	U	H	I	S	D	H	V	I	H
M	S	G	E	S	O	I	E	G	C
A	A	D	D	L	T	H	N	N	I
S	M	J	O	E	T	R	Q	E	R
M	E	F	O	O	D	E	U	R	E
B	Y	N	G	S	F	T	R	V	J

'A man travelling to JERICHO got MUGGED and left for dead. A PRIEST saw him but PASSED BY. So did a LEVITE. But a FOREIGNER from SAMARIA felt SORRY for the man and washed his WOUNDS and took him to an INN for help. He even PAID for the man's FOOD and SHELTER.' This Samaritan was being a GOOD neighbour. We must DO THE SAME.

Luke 10:25-37

Pentecost 16 (2) The Neighbour

ANYONE WHO SAYS HE LOVES GOD BUT HATES HIS BROTHER IS A LIAR!

1 John 4:15-end

I don't remember you having pity on Lazarus in life!

Luke 16:19-end

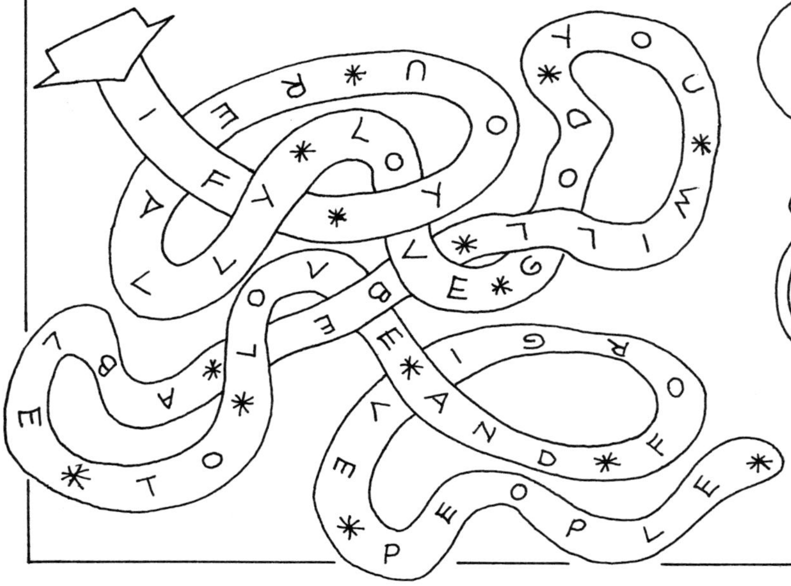

Father Abraham, have pity on me!
Make sure you give help while you still can!

COLOUR THE PICTURE

17th SUNDAY AFTER PENTECOST (TRINITY 16)

Theme: The Proof of Faith

Year 1

Jeremiah 7:1-11; James 1:16-end; Luke 17:11-19

Palm Tree Bible Stories have the story of the ten lepers which can be read aloud to the children today, or the story can be told in your own words. It lends itself well to being acted out, with the help of some sheeting bandages for the lepers which can be flung off as they are healed.

Then talk with the children about when we give presents and enjoy it so much when the person is pleased and thanks us — it draws us closer.

Make a 'thank you' poster by having some pictures of things we want to thank God for, and let each child add to it his own thank you prayer.

Sing: *If I were a butterfly* (ONA, 214).

Year 2

Jeremiah 32:6-15; Galatians 2:15-3:9; Luke 7:1-10

Tell the story of the centurion, using flannelgraph or plasticine models to illustrate it.

Begin with a game of 'Simon Says'. They only obey if Simon gives the order. Talk about who gives orders that are obeyed:

- policemen in traffic;
- teachers at school;
- doctors about medicine;
- Mums and Dads about looking after the home;
- soldiers in battle.

It is necessary for safety and peace to have someone *in charge*.

Now tell the story of the Roman centurion (if possible, have a picture of one commanding his men) showing how he was used to being in charge, and recognised Jesus as being in charge as well. Use a flannelgraph or models to illustrate the story.

Using coloured pencils or pens, let the children decorate these words on a card:

'Lord, I am not worthy to receive you.
But only say the word and I shall be healed.'

Do they recognise it from the communion service? And from the centurion story?

Encourage them to read this from their card next time they are in church and remember how the centurion trusted Jesus to be in charge.

Pentecost 17 (1) The Proof of Faith

DON'T JUST HEAR GOD'S MESSAGE — DO IT!

James 1:16-end

Which ones are living their faith?
The Bible

Q. How many lepers did Jesus heal?
37−27
OR
6+4
OR
OR
98−88
70÷7
OR
Q. How many remembered to say thank you?
½ x 2
OR
8−7
7÷7
OR
OR
¼ x 4

DRAW IN YOUR IDEAS
How can you show God's love this week?

Pentecost 17 (2) The Proof of Faith

WE KNOW CHRIST LIVES IN US WHEN WE CARE FOR OTHERS

1 John 3:14

Luke 7:1-10

H	F	C	O	M	M	A	N	D	H
N	A	L	F	L	K	G	S	O	Y
O	L	O	B	N	L	J	M	R	N
I	O	C	O	F	K	E	P	J	W
R	E	W	Q	I	O	S	W	Z	B
U	D	L	O	U	C	U	R	E	D
T	N	A	V	R	E	S	N	M	X
N	O	F	A	I	T	H	T	D	D
E	N	I	A	G	A	H	C	V	A
C	D	E	Z	A	M	A	Y	O	U

A CENTURION had a SERVANT who was ILL. He sent word to JESUS, 'Sir, I am not WORTHY to have YOU under my ROOF, but just give the COMMAND and I KNOW my servant will be CURED.' Jesus was AMAZED at the man's FAITH. When the messengers got HOME they FOUND the servant completely WELL AGAIN.

The people of Israel were not allowed to live in their own country. Jeremiah believed they would return home one day. How did he show his faith?
He
a
in his own country
and kept the deeds in an
so they would last.

Jeremiah 32:6-15

18th SUNDAY AFTER PENTECOST (TRINITY 17)

Theme: The Offering of Life

Year 1

Deuteronomy 26:1-11; 2 Corinthians 8:1-9; Matthew 5:17-26

Tell the children (or remind them) of how God had helped the people escape from Egypt where they had been slaves, and how, when they reached the promised land, they thanked God every year by bringing a basket of their harvest to his altar. At our harvest festival we do the same. If we remember that God is the provider of all we have, our lives will be rich and full; God holds everything together. Spread out the five sections of this jigsaw puzzle and ask two of the children to make the puzzle up.

If we have God at the centre, all the different parts of our lives can be part of our thanks and praise. Give out pieces of thin card, paper with the puzzle drawn on, scissors, glue and crayons, and help them make their own jigsaws to take home.

My work
My money
GOD
My time
My play

Year 2

Nehemiah 6:1-16 or Ecclesiasticus 38:24-end; 1 Peter 4:7-11; Matthew 25:14-30

Have three boxes with slits in the lids, and some play money. Label the boxes as follows:

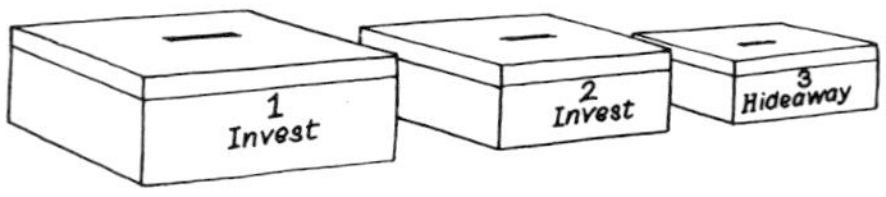
1 Invest
2 Invest
3 Hideaway

Secretly place five pounds inside box 1, two pounds inside box 2 and nothing in box 3.

Tell the children the story of today's Gospel, using more play money. Post five pounds into the first box, two pounds into the second box and one pound into the third.

When you tell the children about the master's return, open each lid. There will now be ten pounds in the first (give him a round of applause), four pounds in the second (another round of applause), and still only one in the last.

Explain how Jesus needs us to use the gifts he gives us, otherwise they will be wasted. Talk with them about their own gifts and things they are good at or advantages they have been given. These may include, for instance, being friendly, strong, a fast runner, musical, clever, artistic, sympathetic, good with animals, a clear reader, funny, or a good listener. They may also include having enough money to share, outgrown toys which could be given away, or time which might be used in helping.

Pentecost 18 (1) The Offering of Life

THE MORE WE GIVE, THE RICHER WE SHALL BE.

2 Corinthians 8:1-9

3
A E
L
P P
S
4
S R
O C
A T
R T
2
E S
R
A P
1
B R
E
A D
DRAW THE HARVEST GIFTS IN THE BASKET

We don't just give at harvest, though.
How are these people giving?
CHARITY RUN
Now draw yourself giving in a kind helpful way.

Deuteronomy 26:1-11

Pentecost 18 (2) The Offering of Life

WHATEVER GIFT YOU HAVE BEEN GIVEN, USE IT FOR THE GOOD OF OTHERS.

1 Peter 4:7-11

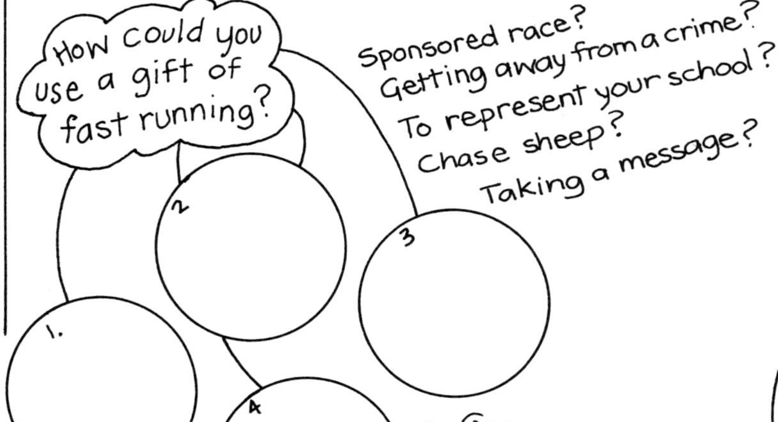

How could you use a gift of fast running?
Sponsored race?
Getting away from a crime?
To represent your school?
Chase sheep?
Taking a message?
1.
2
3
4
Getting to the shops before they close?
(Fill in your ideas)

What are you good at?
How can you best use your gifts?

19th SUNDAY AFTER PENTECOST (TRINITY 18)

Theme: The Life of Faith

Year 1

Genesis 28:10-end; Hebrews 11:1-2, 8-16; Matthew 6:24-end

Make up a story about Mr Worry-a-lot, illustrating it with flannelgraph pictures. He might worry about what he's going to wear, what he's going to eat, who he's going to invite, where he should go on holiday etc.

Then he meets Mr Trust, who finds him in a bad state of nerves. One by one he sorts out Mr Worry-a-lot's problems with him, showing him that he is worrying unnecessarily because God is sure to look after him. When the next worry arises, they remember to stop and ask God to help them and are then much happier, knowing that God will not let them down. You could make the characters look something like this:

Mr Worry-a-lot Mr Trust

and give the children cut-outs of each character to colour in and take home.

Year 2

Daniel 6:10-23; Romans 5:1-11; Luke 19:1-10

Both the Daniel and the Zacchaeus stories provide excellent teaching material. There are many good, sensitive books to use first. Palm Tree has both stories: *Daniel and the Lions* and *Zacchaeus and Jesus*.

After the reading make a model of the story on a base, such as an old tray. Use modelling clay for the figures (and the lions), twigs stuck in cotton reels with tissue paper leaves for trees, painted boxes for houses, sandpaper and stones for the terrain. Bring the finished models in to display in the church with the heading: Trust in God can change your life!

Pentecost 19 (1) The Life of Faith

DON'T WORRY SO MUCH — PUT YOUR TRUST IN GOD.

Matthew 6:24-end

Genesis 28:10-end

Jacob had left home. He was feeling tired and lonely. As he slept, he dreamt about..
He heard God saying "
"
WILL
YOU
SAFE
I
KEEP
Join the dots and colour the picture

"See how your heavenly father feeds the birds and clothes the flowers. Then of course he will look after you as well!"

Pentecost 19 (2) The Life of Faith

GOD WILL KEEP US SAFE; WE CAN TRUST HIM.

Romans 5:1-11

Who is in the pit with Daniel ?
Join the dots and colour the picture

Daniel 6:10-23

Jesus came to save us all.
Zacchaeus, be quick and come down, I must come and stay with you today
He gave Zacchaeus a new way of life.

Luke 19:1-10

20th SUNDAY AFTER PENTECOST (TRINITY 19)

Theme: Endurance

Year 1

Daniel 3:13-26; Romans 8:18-25; Luke 9:51-end

Tell the children the story of Shadrach, Meshach and Abed-nego bringing out their determination to do what they know God wants them to do, even when it puts them in danger. Then help them to make this moving model of the three men in the fire out of card, a lolly stick, sticky tape and colouring pens.

Cut two
Staple together
lolly stick

Year 2

Genesis 32:22-30; 1 Corinthians 9:19-end; Matthew 7:13-27

Bring along two sets of building bricks (not interlocking ones). Divide the children into two groups and let each build a house. One is based on a firm block of wood, the other on a thick layer of sand in a tray.

When both are finished, tell the children Jesus' story of the two houses. At the point of the stormy rain, pour water round the bases of each in turn. The sand will cave in and the 'rock' will not.

Make sure you explain what Jesus told the story for, or they will not understand. Point out how silly it was not to have a good strong foundation, (they may have seen houses being built with foundations deep in the ground) and that we can choose to build our lives on strong rock or slipping sand. Sing *I'm gonna build my life*.

ROCK
SAND

Build on God — put him first

KEEP GOING, DON'T GIVE UP!

Luke 9:51-end

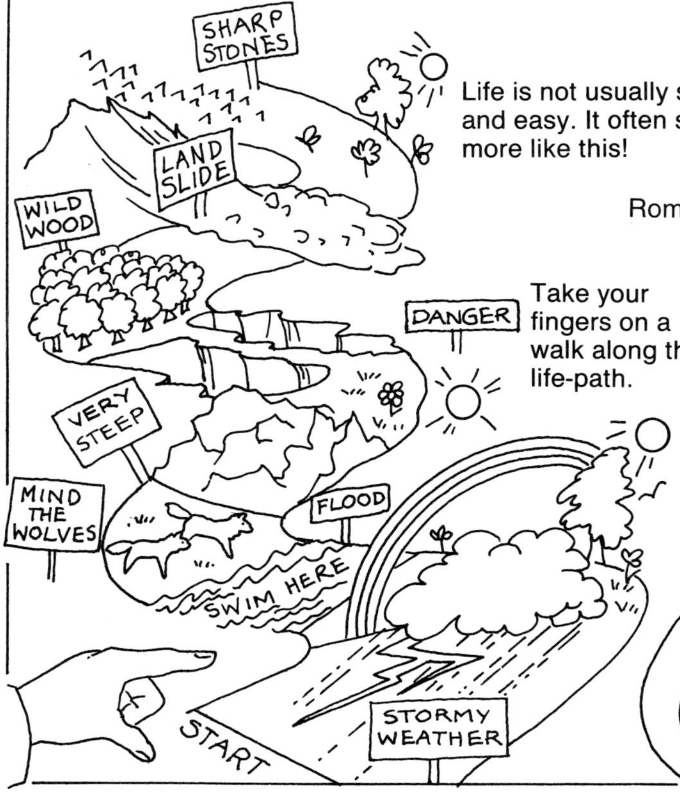
SHARP STONES
LAND SLIDE
WILD WOOD
DANGER
VERY STEEP
MIND THE WOLVES
FLOOD
SWIM HERE
STORMY WEATHER
START

Life is not usually straight and easy. It often seems more like this!

Romans 8:18

Take your fingers on a walk along this life-path.

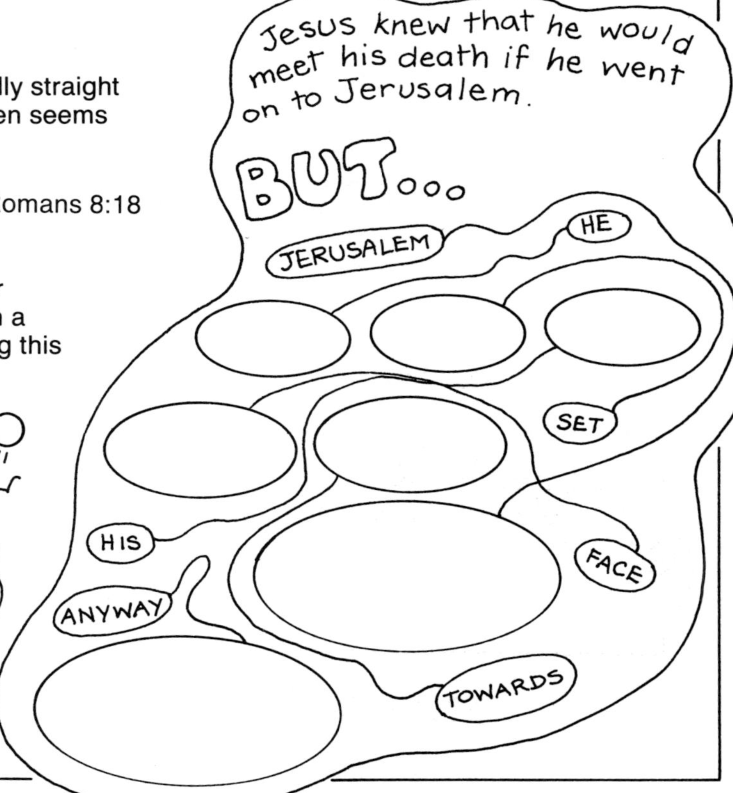
Jesus knew that he would meet his death if he went on to Jerusalem.
BUT...
JERUSALEM
HE
SET
HIS
FACE
ANYWAY
TOWARDS

RUN, THEN, IN SUCH A WAY AS TO WIN THE PRIZE.

1 Corinthians 9:24-25

'If you hear these words of mine and act on them,

U
R
¢
+E
A
who had the sense
2
his
on

How do you get in training for a race?
✗ the wrong ✓ the right and colour in

Matthew 7:24-27

21st SUNDAY AFTER PENTECOST (TRINITY 20)

Theme: The Christian Hope

Year 1

Habakkuk 2:1-4; Acts 26:1-8; Luke 18:1-8

Talk with the children about working hard at something until at last it is finished. They may have found it difficult making a model, mixing a cake, tidying their bedroom or learning to swim or skip, for instance.

You could bring to show them something you had to persevere with, such as a knitted jumper, loaf of bread, or piece of music, and tell them you sometimes wanted to stop and give up, but decided not to.

Help them to see that perseverance is not always easy, but it is always worthwhile.

Now tell the story of Moses, using plasticine models or pictures to illustrate it.

Give each child a card to split into days and with a prayer they have made up to say every day. Perhaps their parents might like to say it with them.

Ask them to bring their cards back next week with a tick drawn each day they remembered to do it.

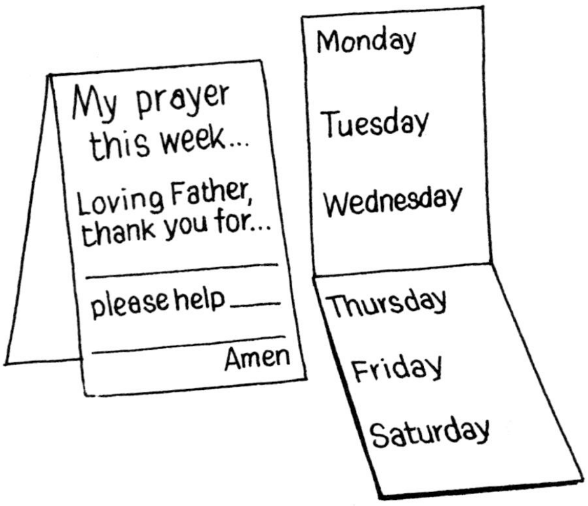
My prayer this week...
Loving Father, thank you for...
please help
Amen
Monday
Tuesday
Wednesday
Thursday
Friday
Saturday

Year 2

Ezekiel 12:21-end; 1 Peter 1:13-21; John 11:17-27

Tell or read the story of today's Gospel. Palm Tree's version is called *Martha, Mary and Lazarus.* Then make a frieze that shows the events and fix it up on the wall in church for everyone to see.

Pentecost 21 (1) The Christian Hope

OUR HOPE FOR HEAVEN IS BASED ON GOD'S PROMISE.

Acts 26:6-7

Draw a picture of something you have been promised

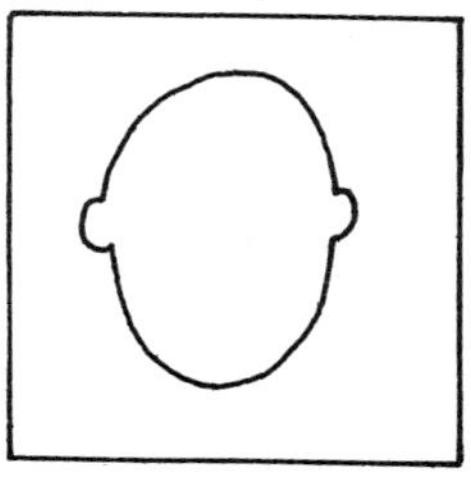

Draw your face when the promise was kept

What has God promised us?

Key:

This:	J	O	Y	A	B	C	E	F	H	I	L
means this:	A	B	C	E	F	H	I	J	L	M	N

This:	M	N	R	S	T	U	V	W	D
means this:	O	R	S	T	U	V	W	Y	G

EB WMT OAHEAUA EL
IA, WMT VEHH CJUA
AUANHJRSELD HEBA
BTHH MB FMW.

Romans 5:2, 5

When?

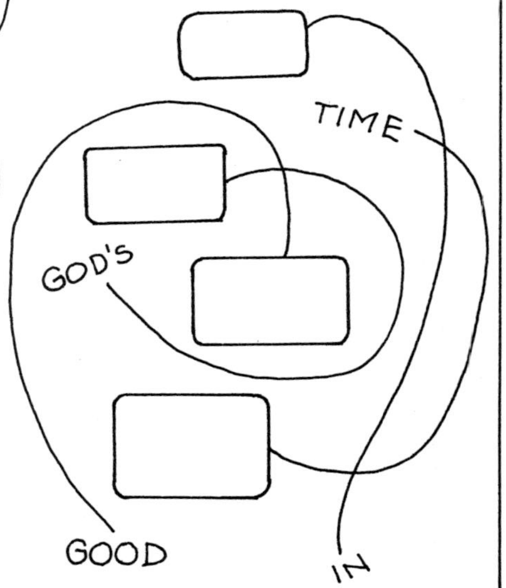

TIME
GOD'S
GOOD
IN

Pentecost 21 (2) The Christian Hope

FIX YOUR HOPES ON CHRIST JESUS.

1 Peter 1:13

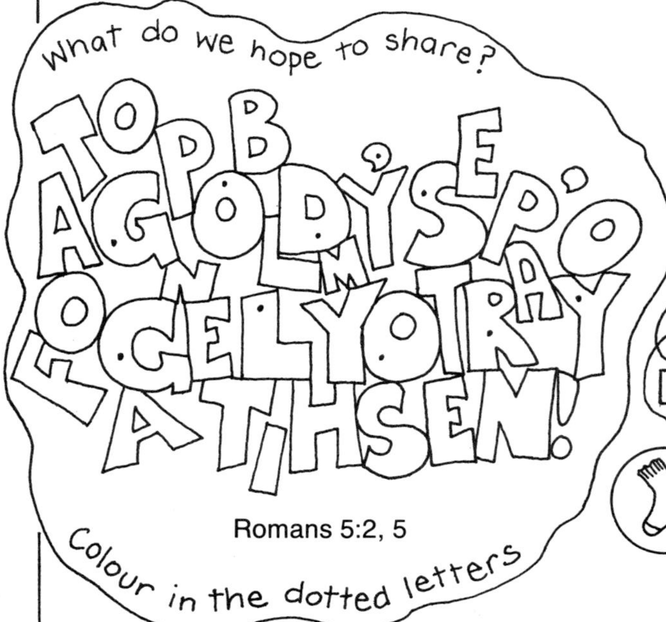

What do we hope to share?
Romans 5:2, 5
Colour in the dotted letters

Jesus says,

22nd SUNDAY AFTER PENTECOST (TRINITY 21)

Theme: The Two Ways

Years 1 and 2

Deuteronomy 11:18-28; 1 John 2:22-end; Luke 16:1-9

First give the children a maze to do, individually with a pencil. Here is one you could use:

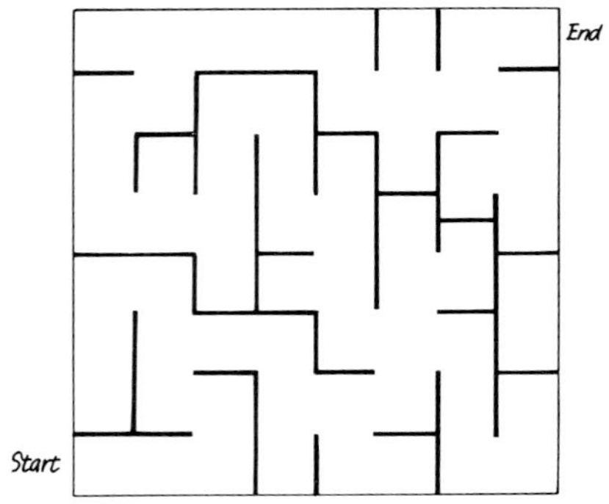

End
Start

Talk about what happens when they go down a dead end:
— they are out of the main route
— they can't make any progress
— the only way out is to retrace their steps
— if they just stay there they may be imprisoned with no freedom.

Now show them a large picture of the maze either on a blackboard or sheet of card. The beginning of our maze, as Christians, is when we are baptised. (Stick a picture of baptism, or a font at the start of the maze.)

All the time we go on the right route we are putting Jesus first. In his love we can enjoy loving Mum and Dad, playing with brothers and sisters, enjoy football, painting, going on holiday, helping Nana, having friends to tea etc. (Write these, and their ideas, in coloured pencil along the route, with a cross, as Jesus' sign, in between each one.) Because Jesus is Love, he helps us love and appreciate other people.

But suppose one thing starts to be more important than our love for Jesus? (Write one item, such as 'football' or 'having friends to tea' at a dead end.) It will cut us off from the supply of Love, and our lives will be stuck at a dead end. So what can we do if that happens? We have to go back the way we came, meet up with Jesus, and then we can live in his love again.

Pentecost 22 (1/2) The Two Ways

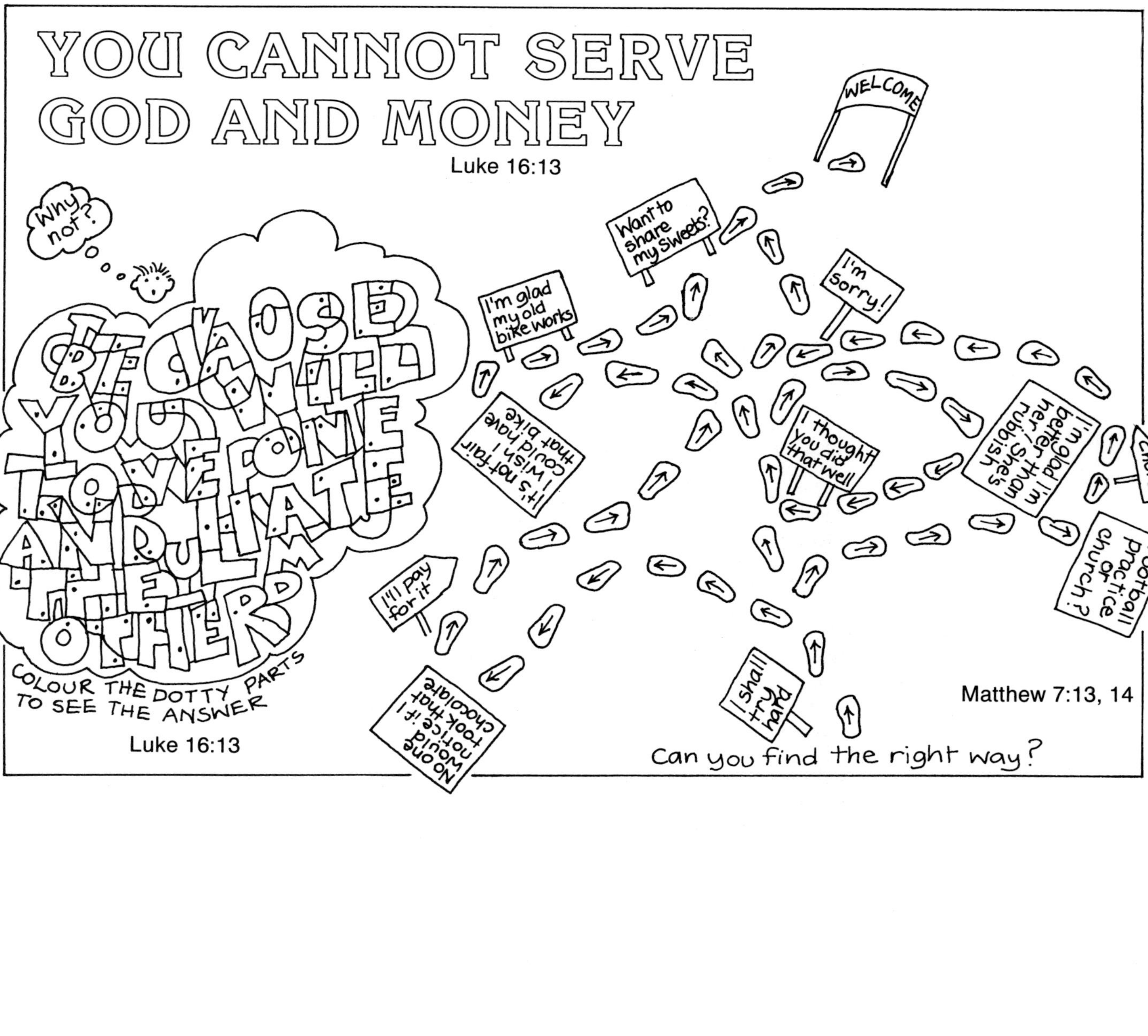

YOU CANNOT SERVE GOD AND MONEY
Luke 16:13
Why not?
COLOUR THE DOTTY PARTS TO SEE THE ANSWER
Luke 16:13
WELCOME
Want to share my sweets?
I'm glad my old bike works
I'm sorry!
It's not fair I wish I could have that bike
I thought you did that well
I'm glad I'm better than her! She's rubbish
Church
Football practice or church?
I'll pay for it
No one would notice if I took that chocolate
I shall try hard
Matthew 7:13, 14
Can you find the right way?

LAST SUNDAY AFTER PENTECOST

Theme: Citizens of Heaven

Year 1

Jeremiah 29:1, 4-14; Philippians 3:7-end; John 17:1-10

If there is an outside area available, this could be used for today's teaching, based on races. If not, have the indoors area clear of chairs and tables for the first part of the session.

Tell the children you are going to have some races, and choose two or three to race first. Have the others cheering at the side lines.

For the next race, give the runners baggy clothes to wear, which will slow them down.

For the third race, have obstacles to get round, over or through. In each case encourage the runners by cheering.

Then gather the children round for prize giving. A nice surprise — everyone who finished gets a prize (small sticker or badge).

Now arrange the chairs in a circle, or several if numbers are large.

Show a large sheet of paper with 'The Race of Life' on it. Talk about what sort of obstacles life has (people nasty to us; moving away from friends; illness etc); how cheering crowds help us (the saints, other people, and we can cheer on others); how the heavy clothes and baskets in our life are our sins (being greedy, unkind, selfish, wishing for what we cannot have, being lazy) so that they relate their races to life. Now each child can make a plasticine model of him or herself running, and put it somewhere along the track.

THE RACE OF LIFE
START
Cheering crowds of saints help us
Life is not always easy
£
Our sins slow us down
FINISH
Well done, you have been good and faithful!

Year 2

Isaiah 33:17-22; Revelation 7:2-4, 9-end; Matthew 25:1-13

Tell the children today's Gospel, making it clear that it is a story Jesus told, not a real event. To help in the telling, have two strips of card, each with five bridesmaids on it.

Wick
Flame
Pull
Keep
my
lamp
burning
Lord

Five have extra oil in a flask, five do not. At the point where the lamps go out, pull the strip along, so that the wicks show instead of the flames.

When they have heard the story and what it tells us about keeping ourselves ready for Jesus, the children can make their own strip of bridesmaids with flames that go out. Write on each: 'Keep my lamp burning Lord' with one word on each bridesmaid. See 'The Dance of the Bridesmaids' on page 128.

FOR US, OUR HOMELAND IS IN HEAVEN.

Philippians 3:20-21

Revelation 7:2-4, 9-end

No one knows what it will look like exactly, but here are some things we DO know!
Everyone will be full of joy
There will be no sadness
No one will hate or fight
GOD IS THERE
We will understand things at last
There will be nothing evil there
Everyone will feel completely at home
It will never end
COLOUR EACH ONE A DIFFERENT COLOUR

Do you have an idea of what heaven is like? Draw and colour it as well as you possibly can.

Dance of the Bridesmaids

Ten bridesmaids, with long dresses and flowers in their hair, carry their lamps during this dance. The lamps are small bowls with nightlights inside.

As the music begins they dance up the centre in two lines of five, doing basically a quick waltz step but free within this to turn and sway or join hands sometimes in pairs. They adjust their hair, smooth each other's dresses, check their lamps in an atmosphere of excited preparation.

Gradually they start to fidget and yawn, resting in different positions — some leaning, some sitting, some lying down. The lamps go out.

From the back comes the trumpet call to announce that the bridegroom will soon be here. The bridesmaids nudge each other awake, flutter about getting neat again, and then the five with extra oil mime their refuelling. The other five kneel and beg them to lend some oil, which the first five refuse to do, pointing out where the oil can be bought.

The five foolish bridesmaids scamper (in contrast to their waltzing) off to buy oil, as the bridegroom, bride and guests come in grand procession up the centre.

The wise bridesmaids dance down to greet him, curtsey and light the way to the centre front. As the bridegroom goes to 'close' the door, the foolish bridesmaids run up with their lamps alight again, but are turned away and walk to the back, dejected, and looking wistfully behind them at the others enjoying themselves.

Handel's *Water Music* has three sections which reflect the three moods of this parable.